Machado de Assis

Twayne's World Authors Series

Latin American Literature

David Foster, Editor
Arizona State University

TWAS 809

Machado de Assis (1839-1908). *Courtesy of Abril Educação of São Paulo, from the series Literatura Comentada.*

Machado de Assis

By Earl E. Fitz

The Pennsylvania State University

Twayne Publishers
A Division of G. K. Hall & Co. • Boston

Machado de Assis
Earl E. Fitz

Copyright 1989 by G. K. Hall & Co.
All rights reserved.
Published by Twayne Publishers
A Division of G. K. Hall & Co.
70 Lincoln Street
Boston, Massachusetts 02111

Copyediting supervised by Barbara Sutton
Book production by Gabrielle B. McDonald
Book design by Barbara Anderson

Typeset in 11 pt. Garamond
by Compositors Typesetters, Cedar Rapids, Iowa

Printed on permanent/durable acid-free paper
and bound in the United States of America

Library of Congress Cataloging-in-Publication Data
Fitz, Earl E.
        Machado de Assis / by Earl E. Fitz.
            p.   cm. — (Twayne's world authors series; TWAS 809. Latin American literature)
        Bibliography: p.
        Includes index.
        ISBN 0-8057-8244-3
        1. Machado de Assis, 1839–1908—Criticism and interpretation.
    I. Title.   II. Series.
    PQ9697.M18Z633   1989
    869.3—dc19   88-25925
                                                                              CIP

To my wife, Julianne, and to our children, Ezra, Caitlin, Dylan, and Duncan.

Also to professors Raymond Sayers and Gregory Rabassa, both of whom taught me to appreciate Machado's artistry.

Contents

About the Author

Earl E. Fitz is Professor of Portuguese, Spanish, and Comparative Literature at The Pennsylvania State University. He is the author of *Clarice Lispector* (Twayne, 1985) and of numerous other articles and monographs (including one comparing Machado de Assis and Henry James) in Brazilian, Spanish American, and comparative literature. Professor Fitz, who is also interested in problems of Inter-American literature and literary relations, is currently working on a book-length study of the development of literature in English and French Canada, the United States, Spanish America, and Brazil. In addition to his teaching duties and scholarly interests, Professor Fitz also serves as an associate editor for the journal *Comparative Literature Studies* and as a member of the advisory board for *Brasil/Brazil*.

Preface

Machado de Assis (1839–1908) is almost certainly the most written about author in all of Brazilian literature. Widely lauded for his novels and short stories, Machado was also a prolific poet, dramatist, translator, literary critic, and social commentator. Although he has long been hailed as Brazil's greatest writer, international recognition has been rather slow to come. Owing undoubtedly to the relative paucity of college level courses dealing with Brazilian literature, Machado de Assis is that extraordinary case of a distinguished artist who has been egregiously overlooked by the vast majority of those who consider themselves knowledgeable about Western literature. This unfortunate situation has been changing in recent years, however, thanks largely to the increasing number of fine translations of Machado's work available. With, sadly, Portuguese still not widely perceived as an important literary language, it has fallen to translators to bring Machado's brilliance to the international audience it so richly deserves. Happily, their labor is proving successful; slowly but ineluctably, Machado is being accorded his rightful place as one of Western literature's major narrativists, a writer whose technical innovations and thematic concerns show him to be an important link between Flaubert's realism and Joyce's modernism.

The objective of this study is twofold: to show that Machado de Assis deserves recognition as a novelist and story writer of primary importance in the late nineteenth/early twentieth century (particularly in terms of the advent of Modernism), and to place him in a comparative context with other, better known contemporary masters such as Henry James, Guy de Maupassant, Anton Chekhov, and Sigmund Freud. Also discussed are the various influences on Machado's art—works and authors as diverse as Sterne's *Tristram Shandy,* Dante, the French romantics, the Greek and Latin classics, Cervantes, and Shakespeare.

An additional goal of this study is to provide, in a single volume, an overview of and critical commentary on all aspects of Machado's work—his famous novels and short stories as well as his less well-known poetry, drama, and translation work; his writings on literary theory and criticism; and his many "crônicas," or chronicles. This is the first English-language work on Machado de Assis to attempt a comprehensive coverage of his life and oeuvre.

This study utilizes the techniques of both comparative literary scholarship and those of close textual analysis. It is hoped that by making use of this dual yet complementary approach to Machado's art the reader will gain a better appreciation of both the excellence of certain individual texts and of his place in the history of Western letters.

A third feature of this study perhaps also deserves special mention (if only to forewarn the reader). Because of certain integral elements in their style, structuring, and critically self-conscious modes of presentation, many of Machado's finest narratives, those from his post-1880 period especially, typify the kind of writing often associated with poststructuralist or deconstructive literary analysis. By focusing on a number of key novels and stories, I have tried to show how the theories of such commentators as Roland Barthes, Jacques Derrida, Paul de Man, Jonathan Culler, and Wolfgang Iser can be illuminatingly applied to Machado's ironic, metaphoric, and metafictional texts. I pay particular attention to the "openness" of many of Machado's most highly regarded novels and stories, including *Epitaph of a Small Winner,* *Dom Casmurro,* "The Psychiatrist," "The Companion," and "Midnight Mass," and to showing how these famous texts generate their semantically balanced ambiguity, their wry self-consciousness and their ontological power.

Even if this study serves only as a general introduction to this too-little-appreciated Brazilian master, its writing will have been justified. My hopes for this study, then, are considerably less acerbic than are those of Braz Cubas, the deceased narrator of *Epitaph of a Small Winner,* who introduces his story by saying, "The book must suffice in itself: if it please you, excellent reader, I shall be rewarded for my labor; if it please you not, I shall reward you with a snap of my fingers, and good riddance to you."

                                                                      Earl E. Fitz

The Pennsylvania State University

Acknowledgments

I would like to thank the following presses for granting permission to quote from works under their copyright: Farrar, Straus & Giroux, Inc.; the Bard Press; the University of California Press, Random House; and the University of Texas Press. I am also indebted to Abril Educação of São Paulo (and to their series, Literatura Comentada) for the frontispiece photograph of the traditional portrait of Machado de Assis.

Special thanks also go to the Department of Spanish, Italian, and Portuguese and the Department of Comparative Literature of The Pennsylvania State University for their encouragement; to Twayne field editor David W. Foster, whose advice and counsel were invaluable; and, finally, to Karen Connelly, who graciously took care of the seemingly endless revisions in preparing the text.

I have used English titles in the text where works are available in English.

I have relied upon the work of many scholars who have dealt with Machado de Assis, perhaps the most written-about author of Brazilian literature, and I trust that my sources have been duly indicated. If I have failed to do so at any point, I apologize, for this was not intentional. Indeed, I should like here to applaud the efforts of all the commentators who have so admirably advanced the case of Machado de Assis. Parabéns to all!

Chronology

1839   Machado de Assis born in a lower middle-class section of Rio de Janeiro (Liberation Hill) on 21 June.

1841   Sister Maria born.

1845   Maria dies in measles epidemic.

1849   Mother dies of tuberculosis.

1854   Father remarries; Machado spends a great deal of time in the bookshop and publishing house of Paula Brito, who befriends him; also frequents a public lending library; begins to write in earnest, working in several different genres.

1855   First published literary effort, a poem, "Ela" (She), in the journal *Marmota Fluminense* 10 January 1855.

1856   Secures a job as an apprentice printer in the Imprensa Nacional, which was then managed by the eminent novelist Manuel Antônio de Almeida, for whom becomes protégé; publishes first piece of literary criticism (on modern comedy; "Idéias vagas—A comédia moderna," *Marmota Fluminense*, 4, 6 September.

1857   Around 1857 begins to write for the theater; many of the plays, all but one comedies, have been lost; also writes poetry, biography, literary theory, and criticism; opera librettos, and does translation work (from French into Portuguese); *A ópera das janelas* (a comic libretto and possibly the first attempt at theater; never produced; text lost).

1858   Publishes his first piece of fiction (a comic short story), "Três tesouros perdidos" (Three lost treasures), 5 January; takes job as cashier and proofreader in Paula Brito's bookstore and publishing company.

1859   Three-act opera *Pipilet* (based on his adaptation of Eugène Sue's novel, *Les mystères de Paris*) presented 24 November.

1860   *Madalena* (a novelette) appears in the journal, *Marmota Fluminense;* becomes an editor for the republican paper *Diário do Rio de Janeiro;* begins to write for the *Semana*

Ilustrada (1860–76) and for other influential journals and papers; *Hoje avental, amanhã luva,* first published play (a one-act comedy; never performed).

1861   Sees an early essay, "A queda que as mulheres têm para os tolos" (which Helen Caldwell believes to be based on Champcenetz's "Petit traité de l'amour des femmes pour les sots"), become his first published book; *Desencantos* (a never performed "dramatic fantasy"); *As bodas de Joaninha,* a one-act operetta, presented in Rio 8 July.

1862   Becomes a censor for the Conservatório Dramático Brasileiro; *O caminho da porta* and *O protocolo* (both one-act comedies) produced in Rio; *Gabriela* (a two-act drama) produced in São Paulo.

1863   *Quase ministro* (a comedy); *As fôrcas caudinas* (play; written between 1859 and 1864; it is not known whether it was ever performed on stage).

1864   *Crisálidas (Chrysalises;* first book of poems); father dies; *O pomo de discórdia,* a three-act comedy, submitted to the Conservatório Dramático Brasileiro; translation of a French comedy, O. Feuillet's *Montjoye,* presented;

1865   Translation of *Suplice d'une femme,* a three-act drama by Girardin and Dumas fils, presented; comedy *Os deuses de casaca* (written in Alexandrine verse) presented; founding member of the Rio literary society, the "Arcádia Fluminense."

1866   Completes three-volume translation of Victor Hugo's novel, *Les travailleurs de la mer;* Portuguese translation of *The Barber of Seville* produced, as well as translation of a five-act French drama by Barrière and Plouvier.

1867   Becomes assistant to the director of the *Diário Oficial;* collaborates with the poet Joaquin Serra and the musician Arthur Napoleão on a four-act, eight-tableaux musical, *O remorso vivo;* translation of Sardou's comedy *La famille benoiton* presented.

1869   Marries Carolina Augusta, sister of recently deceased Portuguese poet and friend Faustino Xavier de Novais; couple resides in Rio; *Contos fluminenses* (Stories of Rio de Janeiro), first collection of short stories.

1870 *Falenas* (Moths)

1872 *Ressurreição* (Resurrection), first novel.

1873 Becomes first officer of the Ministry of Agriculture: *Histórias da meia-noite* (Midnight stories).

1874 *The Hand and the Glove*

1875 *Americanas* (Americana)

1876 *Helena;* appointed section chief of the Ministry of Agriculture.

1878 *Iaiá Garcia; O bote de rapé* (play); *Antes da missa* (play); seriously ill and exhausted, departs Rio late in 1878 for Nova Friburgo to recuperate.

1879 Returns to Rio in March.

1880 *Tu só, tu, puro amor* (You only, you, pure love).

1881 *Epitaph of a Small Winner* (book form); begins to write for the "Gazeta de Notícias."

1882 *Papéis avulsos* (Miscellaneous papers)

1884 *Histórias sem data* (Undated stories)

1888 By imperial decree, is made a member of the Order of the Rose.

1889 Becomes Director General of the Ministry of Agriculture

1891 *Philosopher or Dog?*

1893 Named Director General of Transportation

1896 *Várias histórias* (Various stories); *Não consultes médico* (comedy).

1897 Unanimously elected (in perpetuity) first president of the Brazilian Academy of Letters, of which he was a founding member.

1899 *Páginas recolhidas* (Collected papers).

1900 *Dom Casmurro*

1901 *Poesias completas* (which includes a section of new poems widely known as *Ocidentais,* or Occidentals)

1902 Becomes General Director of Accounts in the Department of Public Roads

1904 Death of beloved wife, Carolina (from intestinal cancer); *Esau and Jacob.*

1906 *Relíquias de casa velha* (Relics from an old house); *Lição de botânica* (comedy).

1908   Dies (of arteriosclerosis complicated by an intestinal disorder
       and cancer of the tongue) 29 September, two months after his
       final novel, *Counselor Ayres' Memorial,* published (in July).

1910   *Outros contos* (Other stories; published posthumously, it in-
       cludes works written between 1864 and 1906 not included in
       earlier anthologies).

Chapter One
Biography and Background

Often described as Brazil's greatest writer, and the first of that nation to achieve international acclaim, Machado de Assis was born in a humble but not entirely disadvantaged section of Rio de Janeiro on 21 June 1839. Machado, as he is known in Brazil, was the firstborn son of Francisco José de Assis, a mulatto house painter from Rio, and Maria Leopoldina Machado de Assis, a Portuguese woman from the Azorean island of São Miguel. While Machado's paternal grandparents were mulatto freed slaves, his godparents, his Excellency Chamberlain Joaquin Alberto de Sousa da Silveira and Dona Maria José de Mendonça Barrozo, were of relatively high social standing, a fact that tends to dispel the widespread notion that Machado was born into circumstances of economic and cultural destitution.

Undoubtedly because Machado was throughout his life reticent about discussing such personal information as his parents, his early struggles with poverty, and his physical ailments (in particular his stuttering, eye problems, and epilepsy), the facts of his life are difficult to discern. Complicating the biographical problems caused by the paucity of reliable information, especially about Machado's difficult early years, has been the development of a number of myths and legends about his identity as a person and an artist. In spite of these uncertainties, however, as Helen Caldwell, Araripe Júnior, Afrânio Peixoto, and others have shown—and as Machado de Assis himself indicated in a number of letters and articles—certain features of his life seem indisputable. He was, as Caldwell sums up, "an intellectual; a courteous gentleman; a patriot; a devoted husband; a hard working, steady, law-abiding citizen and public servant; drank tea instead of something stronger; an honest man in every sense of the word; a great reader but also gregarious; a 'joiner' of both political and literary societies; a man given to warm friendships, fond of animals, children, whist, chess, dancing, music, theater and conversation; and above all a man of infinite good taste."[1]

At the same time, however, there are the fallacious and derogatory stories about Machado, those that allege he was "a cold, churlish, self-centered eccentric, quick to take offense, given to biting sarcasm, a prude, a social climber, indifferent to the welfare of his country and his fellowmen, timid and withdrawn because of a feeling of inferiority over his Negro blood and impoverished childhood as son of a Negro laborer and Negro washerwoman, that he was gloomy and sickly, stammered unmercifully, and staggered from epileptic fit to epileptic fit, that he abandoned his stepmother and had affairs with actresses—not very good actresses."[2]

As scholars unearth more and more information about Machado's early years, however, it has become clear that the true portrait of the man hews much closer to the positive view than the negative, which seems to have been based on hearsay evidence, rumor, textual misreadings, and professional jealousies. Ironically, this unflattering view of Machado may have also been fueled by Machado himself, who throughout his life was reluctant to set the biographical record straight.

Devoted to his art, to what his contemporary Henry James would call the craft of fiction, Machado repeatedly maintained in his prefaces, his personal correspondence, and his newspaper columns that his true identity lay within his work and that, with the exception of his last novel, *Counselor Ayres' Memorial* (which Machado acknowledged to have been heavily influenced by the memory of his deceased wife), his life had no bearing on his fiction.[3] Yet in spite of these protestations Machado's work has often been evaluated biographically, in a futile attempt to explain his themes, characters, forms, and styles in terms of his early penury, his mixed racial heritage, his epilepsy, his stammering, his sedate family life, his gregarious social life, and his exemplary career as a civil servant.[4] For Machado a crucial principle of art was that it can and should exist on its own, independent of its maker, an aesthetic stance that perhaps explains why he was so adamant about not wanting his work—his art—analyzed in terms of his life.

But biographical criticism was the norm during Machado's lifetime, which helps us understand both why Machado's work (his post-1880 narratives and poems, especially) was so puzzling to the public as well as to his loyal supporters, and why Machado has had to wait until the mid and late twentieth century to begin to enjoy the international acclaim he deserves. A grand anachronism, Machado was, in terms of the technical innovations he wrought upon the novel and the short story form, far ahead of his time, and it has only been in the second half of the twentieth century that his numerous narrative innovations have been duly recognized. In many ways, as the American novelist John Barth says, Machado seems both modernistic and even postmodernistic, a writer whose fine sense of irony and whose awareness of the technical possibilities inherent in the metafictional author/narrator/ reader/implied reader relationships make him seem more an artist of the

1960s or 1970s, for example, than of the late nineteenth and early twentieth century.[5]

A celebrated if perplexing and controversial author, Machado de Assis enjoyed a long and fruitful career, one that produced nine novels, four collections of poetry, more than two hundred short stories, numerous translations, several theatrical productions (many of which have been lost), hundreds of pages of newspaper columns and "crônicas" (nonfictional commentaries on a variety of subjects), literary theory and criticism, and a voluminous personal correspondence. So extensive and outstanding is Machado's literary corpus that one critic, Emir Rodríguez Monegal, has called it "unrivaled in Latin American letters."[6]

Although there is some question about the validity of doing so, scholars have traditionally divided Machado's career into two parts, pre-1880 and post-1880. The earlier works, chief among which are the poetry collections *Crisálidas* (1864: Chrysalises), *Falenas* (1870; Moths) and *Americanas* (1875; Americana), the story collections *Contos fluminenses* (1869; Stories of Rio de Janiero) and *Histórias da meia-noite* (1873; Midnight stories) and the novels *Ressurreição* (1872; Resurrection), *The Hand and the Glove* (1874), *Helena* (1876), and *Iaiá Garcia* (1878), are essentially romantic in nature. Written under the influence of several different French authors, including Victor Hugo, whose *travailleurs de la mer* Machado had translated in 1866, these entertaining and popular early works deal typically with rather bland and conventional middle-class love affairs. Mildly ironic and occasionally melodramatic, the pre-1880 pieces show little or nothing of the fierce social satire and philosophic skepticism that infuse the later works.

The early poems, too, exhibited predominantly romantic themes and techniques. By 1859, five years before his first book of poems, *Crisálidas,* was published, Machado, as L. C. Ishimatsu notes, "had become acquainted with the works of the French Romantics—Musset, Vigny, Hugo, Lamartine, and Dumas," who were, in addition to several Portuguese and Brazilian poets of the time, the principal influences on his early verse.[7] Even one of Machado's later poetic works, *Americanas* (1875) was romantic in that a majority of its poems dealt with the American Indian, a popular romantic subject. *Americanas,* in fact, has been called "the last major example of Indianist poetry" written during Brazil's romantic period.[8]

In late 1878, exhausted from years of intense work and suffering from several physical maladies, including eye problems and recurring intestinal infections, Machado, in the company of his wife, Carolina, left Rio for three months to rest and recuperate in the nearby mountain resort city of Nova Friburgo. Returning to Rio in March of 1879, Machado de Assis was, if not a changed man (as many critics have suggested), then at least a changed writer, one who no longer felt encumbered by the stale conventions of romanticism and anxious to break new ground. Although there is some truth to the argument advanced by such critics as Afrânio Coutinho and José Veríssimo (who, as a young writer and critic, had been befriended by Machado de Assis) that the germ of the "late" (post-1880) Machado was present in the "early" (pre-1880) writer, one also feels that Machado's post-1880 work is highly unique, an eclectic body of literature that shows the influence of numerous authors and aesthetic concepts but one that defies any kind of critical pigeonholing.[9]

Increasingly successful in narrative, as opposed to either poetry or drama, Machado unquestionably produced his best work during the years from 1880, the year *Epitaph of a Small Winner* was first published (in serial form via the *Revista Brasileira*), to 1908, the year *Counselor Ayres's Memorial* appeared, some two months before his death at age sixty-nine. These post-1880 works, representing the so-called "mature" Machado de Assis, include the following: the novels, *Epitaph of a Small Winner* (1880 serialized version; 1881 book version); *Philosopher or Dog?* (1891); *Dom Casmurro* (1900); *Esau and Jacob* (1904); and *Counselor Ayres' Memorial* (1908); the short story collections, *Papéis avulsos* (1882; Miscellaneous papers); *Histórias sem data* (1884; Undated stories); *Várias histórias* (1896; Various stories); *Páginas recolhidas* (1899; Collected papers); and *Relíquias de casa velha* (1906; Relics from an old house); *Outros contos* (Other stories), a collection of stories published posthumously but written between 1864 and 1906; and the volume of poetry, *Poesias completas* (1901; Complete poems), which includes a section of verses widely known under the title, *Ocidentais* (Occidentals).

Although one can find certain thematic, stylistic, and characterizational ties between the pre- and post-1880 Machado, it is also true, as Jack Schmitt and Lorie Ishimatsu observe, "There is little in Machado's early novels and stories to prepare the reader for the abrupt changes in content and technique found in *Epitaph of a Small Winner* . . . , his first great novel, and *Miscellaneous Papers* . . . , the first of five volumes in which the majority of his best stories appear."[10] These later works, in particular the narratives, also show Machado moving away from the influence of the French romantics and toward that of certain English writers, most notably Shakespeare, Fielding, and Sterne, though many other authors, such as Swift, Voltaire, Cervantes, Pascal, and Dante, were also exerting a significant influence on him.[11] The Machado de Assis of this period was an artist who, like Shakespeare, tended to create characters who represented certain national types and characteristics

and yet who, in their complexity and humanity, attained truly universal pro-
portions. In three of Machado's best-known novels, for example, *Epitaph of
a Small Winner, Philosopher or Dog?*, and *Dom Casmurro*, and in stories like
"The Psychiatrist," "The Education of a Stuffed Shirt," and "The Animal
Game," he succeeds brilliantly in expanding the particulars of a definitively
and realistically portrayed Brazilian scene into a general, all-encompassing
commentary on the human experience.

Like all great writers Machado makes the local express the universal, time-
less truths about how and why we live out our lives as we do. By working in
this fashion Machado was able to create, especially in his later narratives (narrative being the métier in which he shows his true genius), works of art that
offer both a wealth of incisive yet always implicit sociopolitical criticism of the
Brazil of the Second Empire (1840–90) and an acerbic commentary on the
human condition. A subtle yet compellingly philosophic writer, Machado de
Assis is also a profoundly Brazilian writer, one, however, who constantly chal-
lenges his reader to realize that for however much his characters are distinc-
tively Brazilian, they never cease to be human, to be emblematic of a larger
enigma, that of existence itself. The Machado de Assis who left, therefore,
the artfully done but basically tepid love intrigues of novels like *The Hand
and the Glove* and *Iaiá Garcia* for the cutting irony, social satire, and arguably pessimistic world view so prevalent in works like *Epitaph of a Small Winner* and *Philosopher or Dog?* is one and the same man, a gifted artist whose
capacious sense of art and reality has made him one of the Western tradition's
greatest if ignored writers.

Who, then, was Machado de Assis? What were the facts of his life and art
that allow us to know him as a man and an artist? We know that he was a mulatto, born 21 June 1839, into humble but not poverty-ridden circumstances in what might be described as a lower middle-class section of Rio de
Janeiro called "O Morro do Livramento" ("Liberation Hill"). We know, too,
that Machado was a man who had both a private and a public side to his personality and that he was a writer devoted first and foremost to the integrity of
his art. Yet his was no ivory tower existence, as many have alleged. On the
question of race relations, for example, Machado de Assis was an artist not
only conscious of the injustices suffered by black people in Brazil but in his
own way one actively engaged in the struggle against slavery. Though these
social concerns are most apparent in works like *Epitaph of a Small Winner*
and *Counselor Ayres' Memorial*, they are present directly and indirectly in
Machado's other works as well. The key point about Machado's concern over
slavery, an issue that serves very well to illustrate the nature of his many civic,
social, and political concerns, is that while he was keenly aware of being not

only a mulatto but a citizen of a culture based on slavery, he never wrote as a "Black Writer." Although, according to Antônio Cândido, Machado himself did not encounter a great deal of overt racial prejudice in his life until he made plans to marry a white Portuguese woman whose family opposed the match (it apparently did not matter to her), he was certainly aware of the inequalities, racial and otherwise, that troubled his society.[12] In terms of Machado's social conscience, we do well to remember in sum that, as Maria Luisa Nunes puts it, "he was more concerned with the perfection of his art than with taking a militant stand in social causes. Nevertheless, he took his stand on the issues and his perception of them was far sighted enough to comprehend more than their immediate implications. . . . He did not wish perhaps to be known as a black, white, or mulatto artist but as an artist."[13]

Owing undoubtedly to the impecunious circumstances of his family, Machado, who attended a school in Rio's São Cristóvão district, never received anything more than an elementary school education. Because his formal schooling was so limited, one of the great and as yet unresolved questions about Machado's career is how he came by all the literary, philosophic, and artistic allusions that permeate his work. It seems fair to say that Machado de Assis, an epileptic, stammering, and disadvantaged mulatto from a run-down part of mid-nineteenth-century Rio de Janeiro, was an authentic genius, a man who overcame tremendous odds to become one of the greatest writers of his age. Almost entirely self-taught, Machado made frequent visits as a boy to the Library of the Portuguese Cabinet of Reading, which opened new vistas to him. He was a voracious reader, one who not only remembered what he read but who evaluated, assimilated, and transformed it as well. He appears to have been drawn to the literary milieu even as a boy of fifteen, when, with his mother dead, his four-year-old sister, Maria, dead (in the measles epidemic of 1845) and his father remarried, he began to make his own way in the closely knit world of Brazil's publishing industry. Showing an early and precocious fascination with the world of letters, Machado, even as an adolescent, engaged himself not only in an extensive and eclectic reading program but in literary composition as well. While still in his teens he became a serious and respected man of letters.

The year 1855 was a decisive one for the fledgling author because it was then that his first published literary effort appeared, a historically important (but artistically unimpressive) poem, "Ela" (She).[14] Printed in the magazine *Marmota Fluminense,* "Ela" is fully representative in form, theme, and style of the youthful Machado's close attachment to the basic tenets of romanticism, and it reflects his lifelong concern over questions of form and technique.

In 1856 Machado took a job as an apprentice printer with the Imprensa Nacional. While at this post he made the acquaintance of the press's director, Manuel Antônio de Almeida, an important novelist who, recognizing Machado's potential, became his benefactor, friend, and patron. Two years later, in 1858, while translating such romantics as Lamartine and Dumas and while seeing his own work begin to appear in print, Machado became an editor and proofreader (and, apparently, a part-time cashier) with Paula Brito's influential bookstore and publishing house, which put out the journal *Marmota Fluminense,* in which several of Machado's poems had already appeared.

It is around this time that Machado began to cultivate narrative fiction as well as criticism. The essay "Idéias vagas—A comédia moderna" (1856; Random thoughts: on modern comedy) is his earliest published example of the latter genre while his novelette *Madalena* (1860; Madalena), simplistic and rife with romantic clichés, is an example of his early and somewhat clumsy foray into the realm of extended fiction. Two years earlier, in 1858, he had published his first short story, a comic piece entitled "Três tesouros perdidos" (Three lost treasures). The years between 1858 and 1863 then were active ones for Machado, who, using such pen names as Gil, Job, Platão, Vítor de Paula, Lara, and Max, also became a contributor to a number of important journals and papers. His editorial involvement (at the invitation of Quintino Bocaiúva) with the republican paper *Diário do Rio de Janeiro* gives ample evidence of Machado's keen awareness of sociopolitical issues and of his discerning and liberal views.

The late 1850s and early 1860s were also a period in which Machado was busy with writing for and about the theater. Though he never gained fame as a dramatist, Machado like Henry James admired the theatre and worked at it assiduously. And, while he translated several French dramas into Portuguese, he had a strong preference for comedies as well as a fondness for opera. He also wrote several critical and theoretical studies of the relationship between characters and plot in drama, on the need to establish a national theater in Brazil, and on the efficacy of the theater as a vehicle for fomenting social change. Although he wrote less and less for the theater after the early 1870s, he never lost his interest in drama as an art form. Indeed, there is good reason to believe that Machado's early experience as a playwright and drama critic had a significant influence on the form and structure of his later fiction.

By 1870 then Machado de Assis was widely perceived as one of the rising stars of Brazilian literature. Having firmly established himself in all the major literary genres of his time, and having made a name for himself as a critic and literary theoretician, Machado was at age thirty-one well on his way to becoming Brazil's leading man of letters, an honor that only a few years later would be indisputably his. A profilic writer, Machado, between the ages of fifteen and thirty, "composed some 6,000 lines of poetry, 19 plays and opera librettos, 24 short stories, 182 columns and articles, and 17 translations into Portuguese from French and Spanish."[15] But more than merely productive, Machado de Assis was a critically demanding and innovative writer, who grew in skill, scope, and complexity with every effort, particularly in the novel and short story forms.

After marrying in 1869 Carolina Augusta Xavier de Novais, whose brother Faustino, a satiric Portuguese poet, had (until his death in the same year, 1869) been a close friend of Machado, the couple settled in Rio de Janeiro, initially residing on the Rua dos Andradas but eventually (by 1884) at number 18, Rua Cosme Velho.

The early 1870s were also important for Machado because it was at this time that he secured a series of bureaucratic posts with the government, which finally provided him with two benefits he had long needed: a steady, reliable income and, because of the regular hours, substantial amounts of free time, during which he could pursue the great passion of his life—writing. By all accounts, Machado was a model civil servant. Reliable, honest, punctual, and fair-minded, he rose from secretary to the Technological Dictionary Committee of the Navy, a job he took in 1872, to first officer of the Ministry of Agriculture in 1873. In 1876 Machado was named a section chief in this same ministry and in 1889 was made its head. Recognized for his exemplary work, Machado was appointed in 1902 the General Director of Accounts in the Department of Public Roads.

With his domestic and professional life now in order, Machado began during the 1880s and 1890s to produce his greatest works: the extraordinary novel *Epitaph of a Small Winner* (1880), the superb tales of *Papéis avulsos* (1882), *Histórias sem data* (1884), and *Páginas recolhidas* (1899), and in 1900 *Dom Casmurro,* a work that has been called the finest novel ever written in the Americas, North or South.[16] Widely acclaimed as Brazil's premier writer and critic, Machado was in 1897 unanimously elected first president of the Brazilian Academy of Letters, which he had been instrumental in founding the year before. In 1904, however, tragedy struck: Carolina, Machado's beloved wife and companion, passed away 20 October 1904.

In the final published work of his life, the novel *Counselor Ayres' Memorial* (1908), Machado finds a way to transform his memory of Carolina into an artistically refined statement about the ennobling effect the qualities of love, respect, and fidelity have on human existence. Acknowledging to friends that one of the novel's principal characters, Carmo, was based on his vision of

Carolina, Machado de Assis wrote in *Counselor Ayres' Memorial* both a technically sophisticated text and a poignant paean to life and love. Another of his critically overlooked efforts, it is perhaps his most moving.

Though mentally full of energy and perhaps even planning to begin a new novel,[17] Machado's own health began to fail in the spring of 1908. Wracked by increasingly frequent and severe intestinal infections and suffering from a cancerous ulcer on his tongue, Machado could no longer consume solid foods. On 21 August he attended his final session of the Brazilian Academy. Said to be an agnostic, Machado declined to have a priest present during his final hours. Death came at 3:45 A.M. on 29 September 1908. On the death certificate the cause of death is listed as arteriosclerosis. In accordance with his wishes, Machado was laid to rest alongside his wife, Carolina, in Rio's São João Batista Cemetery.

Chapter Two

Machado de Assis and the Western Tradition: A Comparative Approach

When we think of the development of the modern novel in the Western tradition, we ordinarily think of such writers as Cervantes, Henry Fielding, Sir Walter Scott, Charles Dickens, Gustave Flaubert, James Joyce, Marcel Proust, and Thomas Mann. For well over two hundred years, the novel, that most protean of literary genres, has occupied a central place in Western literature. The names we associate with its evolution, from *Don Quixote* (pt. 1, 1605; pt. 2, 1615) to *Ulysses* (1922), rank among the most celebrated of our tradition. Absent among these names, however, is that of Machado de Assis, an iconoclastic novelist and short story writer who, thanks largely to the medium of translation, is only now gradually being "discovered" as one of the outstanding narrativists of the late nineteenth and early twentieth century.

A question, therefore, arises: why has it taken so long for Machado to begin to receive the international acclaim he deserves? Though many factors are involved, the answer to this question is a function of two interrelated issues: language and canon. Portuguese, Machado's supple vehicle of expression, is simply not widely recognized as a literary language in which quality literature is written. Though it is currently the sixth most widely spoken language in the world, ranking well ahead of such better-known tongues as German, French, Italian, and Japanese, Portuguese is not commonly studied. As a consequence, its literature remains a terra incognita to the vast majority of readers and critics, including those who pride themselves on being knowledgeable about the Western literary tradition. While the literature of Spanish America has in general, especially since World War II, attained the international recognition it deserves, the literature of Brazil, the largest, wealthiest, and most populous nation in Latin America, has been largely ignored, left to languish in a kind of cultural limbo. Even now, when otherwise careful critics speak of "Latin American" literature, they almost without exception have in mind works only from Spanish America, not Brazil. A literarily invisible giant possessed of a sophisticated and highly unified national literature, Brazil is a nation that is, however, slowly emerging from its isolation. In the literary sphere, the late twentieth-century "discovery" of Machado de Assis is one more bit of evidence that proves the legitimacy of his country's long overdue emergence on the world stage.

Finally, Machado de Assis, a Brazilian writer working in Portuguese, has been neglected because of the restrictive and even exclusionist nature of the Western literary canon. Historically, it has been dominated by European works, which have been established as the models against which other works—even those that are not European or American in origin or inspiration—must be evaluated. Although Machado de Assis labored, culturally and linguistically at least, on the margin of the Western tradition, intellectually and aesthetically he was steeped in it. A voracious and discerning reader, he was intimately acquainted with not only the giants of the Western tradition but with its lesser-known lights as well. It is ironic that a writer so well read in the languages and literatures of the Western tradition should have been so long neglected by readers outside his own time and place. The truth, unfortunately, is that Brazilian literature is not recognized as constituting a significant part of the canon of Western literature. Although ever increasing numbers of comparative studies are helping to correct this problem, Machado, who is still not widely read outside of the ken of Luso-Brazilianists, remains largely ignored, an unrecognized genius. Had he written in French, German, or English, for example, Machado de Assis would be as well-known today as Flaubert, Goethe, or Shakespeare. It is my intention in this chapter to move Machado out of his cultural and linguistic isolation and to place him in the context of other, better known writers of his time.

Where, then, and how, one asks, does Machado de Assis fit into the Western tradition? Chronologically, his life (1839–1908) spans several literary movements—romanticism, realism, naturalism, parnassianism, symbolism, and modernism—that are of immense cultural and artistic significance. Never an unquestioning devotee of any single movement or aesthetic orientation, Machado de Assis was an eclectic writer who, always in quest of a more perfect work of art, borrowed freely from radically different works and periods. Thus, one of his most celebrated novels, *Epitaph of a Small Winner*, exhibits certain features of the eighteenth-century English novel (Laurence Sterne's *Tristram Shandy*, 1760–67, for example, was a work that exerted a significant influence on Machado)[1] at the same time that it anticipates many of the features of the later developing modernist novel. As an active translator, Machado in his pre-1880 era was a kind of literary courier, helping to funnel through the texts he chose to translate (which included works by Eugène Sue, Louis René de Champcenetz, Alexandre Dumas fils, and Hugo) the powerfully influential presence of French romanticism into Brazilian letters. But while Machado had a personal and artistic affinity for certain of romanticism's basic tenets,[2] its penchant for ideals and idealized states of being, for example, he was never totally committed either to romanticism proper or to its aesthetics. Although his pre-1880 novels make use of numerous romantic techniques and motifs, these same works also utilize several technical and thematic features that turn up in more refined form in the later, "realistic" works. And while he heartily disliked "realismo" (which for him was largely synonymous with what, in literary history, is often called naturalism), Machado was fascinated by reality, especially the philosophic and ethical complexities of human existence. Not surprisingly, it is precisely in the area of poetically rendered psychological and philosophic discourse that he accomplished his most brilliant work in the post-1880 years.

To an extraordinary extent an intense and highly poetic use of allegory, symbolism, simile, metaphor, synecdoche, and ironic contrast comes to play an integral role in Machado's post-1880 narratives. Though perplexing to readers and critics of the time, his experimentation with such staples of modernist narrative techniques as fragmentation, ellipsis, and irony, the metaphoric advancement of plot, the manipulation of time, the use of implied readers, unreliable narrators (and narratees), and the insistence that the reader not be passive, that he or she participate actively in the fluid process of textual interpretation, all conspire to show how Machado de Assis was a writer ahead of his time, one who after 1880 was trying out various forms and techniques we now associate with modernist and even postmodernist literature while working, historically, under the (for him) pernicious star of naturalism.[3] If chronologically speaking Machado de Assis belongs primarily to the years spanning romanticism, realism, symbolism, and naturalism, he also anticipates in an aesthetic sense many of the forms, techniques, styles, and themes of the modernists. When read from this perspective, he fits naturally into the age and narrative tradition we associate with Proust, Joyce, and Mann.

A "national writer par excellence,"[4] Machado was undoubtedly the greatest Brazilian writer of his time. Beyond this, he was the first writer of that country to transcend his nationalism and attain a truly universalist dimension. By extrapolating the universal from the local or particular, as he advocates in the 1873 essay "O instinto de nacionalidade" (The instinct of nationality), Machado expresses his "brasilidade," or "Brazilianness," so indirectly and artfully that it seems a perfectly natural microcosm of the eternal human conflicts with which he is primarily interested. Critically and artistically, then, Machado de Assis was the first writer in the history of Brazilian literature to systematically project images of the universal human condition through the lens of Brazilian culture. It is ironic that the first Brazilian writer to free Brazil from its cultural and linguistic isolation has on the stage of world literature been himself a victim of isolation and neglect. A captivating blend of the archaic and avant-garde, Machado de Assis is a grand anachronism, a highly unique and original writer who does not fit his historical time and place.

Like Thomas Hardy, with whom he can be legitimately compared, Machado de Assis shows how the forces of fate, of an indifferent universe, combine with the inconsistent and often contradictory aspects of human nature to undermine and destroy people. Machado's vision of human existence is like Hardy's basically tragic. Much of the humor that permeates Machado's work, and in particular that of his late work, is again like Hardy's darkly ironic in nature. Some interesting parallels can be drawn, for example, between Hardy's *Tess of the D'Urbervilles* (1891) and Machado's *Philosopher or Dog?* (1891). In both cases an intelligent and sensitive protagonist is destroyed by a web of circumstances and events that generate a bitterly ironic view of life. Hardy, moreover, like Machado is often referred to as a "pessimistic" writer, a charge that both authors would dispute by showing through certain of their characters that although we humans are largely at the mercy of the indifferent social, natural, and psychological forces that determine our destiny, we can, at times at least, achieve a kind of personal dignity through endurance, willpower, and perseverance.

Like Herman Melville, whose own bipartite career as a fiction writer has, as Augusto Meyer notes, certain parallels with that of Machado,[5] the Brazilian writer saw through the self-satisfied veneer of his society and created works of art that threw light on its dark, distorted underside. A further parallel between these two writers is that both Melville and Machado de Assis wrote narratives in which the techniques of realism were deliberately combined with those of a rich and mythic symbolism. In *Moby-Dick* (1851) and *Dom Casmurro* (1900), for example, powerfully poetic and allegorical texts are woven around characters, Captain Ahab and Dom Casmurro, who though for different reasons project certain twisted aspects of their personalities onto people and other entities around them. In both cases the attentive reader slowly comes to see that both Ahab and Dom Casmurro, like Braz Cubas (of *Epitaph of a Small Winner*) and Captain Vere (of *Billy Budd*), are either blind to the evil that lurks within them or unwilling to acknowledge it. Each of these four characters undertakes an elaborate and ironic rationalization of his monomaniacal and destructive actions, actions that generate a grimly sardonic sense of life.

Another author of this period with whom Machado can be compared is the belle of Amherst, Emily Dickinson. Like Dickinson Machado was possessed of an intensely compressed poetic style. Many of Machado's most memorable characters exhibit the same kind of painful self-consciousness that we find in Dickinson's best verse. Both Machado and Dickinson deal essentially with themes that extend far beyond the settings of their works and that touch upon the cosmic, eternal problems of human existence such as the ambivalent and paradoxical nature of love, the passage of time, the relationship of life and death, and illusion versus reality. When Dickinson writes in one of her most famous poems, "A Bird came down the Walk— / He did not know I saw— / He bit an Angleworm in halves / And ate the fellow, raw" (number 328), she is expressing, in arch though matter-of-fact language, a conception of an indifferent and capricious universe, of a nature that consists simultaneously of beauty and terror, tranquillity and violence, life and death. This unsettling conception of nature is very similar to the one presented by Machado in such texts as *Epitaph of a Small Winner* (chap. 31, "The Black Butterfly"), *Dom Casmurro* (chap. 17, "The Worms") and *Philosopher or Dog?* (chaps. 200 and 201).

In terms of purely literary works, the influences exerted on Machado de Assis were many and varied, including authors as diverse as Homer, Aeschylus, Xenophanes, Cervantes, Dante, Shakespeare, and Goethe. But though the presence of some of these authors—Dante, Sterne, and Shakespeare, for example—is very strong, Machado's work is "a new and unique synthesis," "the result of his art . . . alone."[6] Comparative studies done by Eugênio Gomes, Clotilde Wilson, Afrânio Coutinho, and others show how other writers and philosophers, including Jonathan Swift (Gomes), Erasmus (Wilson), and Pascal (Coutinho) also had a powerful effect on Machado and his sense of human existence.[7] But though all these influences are undoubtedly valid, the genius of Machado, as for all truly great artists, lies in his ability to synthesize, to take certain features of different writers and thinkers and combine them in new and startling ways, which in their transcendent originality make Machado's work distinctive. Although he hardly ever left his native Rio de Janeiro, Machado de Assis was deeply rooted in the artistic and intellectual achievements of the Western tradition, but as T. S. Eliot in "Tradition and the Individual Talent" (1919) and Harold Bloom in *The Anxiety of Influence* (1973) later said every artist must do, he transformed them into radically new works of art.

The pre-1880 influences on Machado were predominantly those of French romanticism (Hugo, René de Chateaubriand, Sue, Dumas fils, and others), although the work of Honoré de Balzac, Stendhal, and Flaubert should not be discounted, especially during Machado's formative years. Of these latter writers, Stendhal and Flaubert show perhaps the closest affinities with Machado. Stendhal, in fact, is actually cited by Braz Cubas (the deceased narrator and protagonist of *Epitaph of a Small Winner*) in the wry "To The Reader" section that opens his novel, the implication being that both Braz and Machado were thoroughly acquainted with Stendhal's work.[8] Renowned for his psychological insight, his presentation of the ethical values of his society, his fascinating characters, and his sharp, vivid style, Stendhal was like Machado also keenly interested in the psychology of love, particularly its unsentimentalized aspects. Though not dissected, Stendhal's characters like Machado's reveal themselves from the inside out and in so doing give the reader a sense of gaining an illusion-free view of their society. Thus, both Stendhal and Machado capture the essence of their respective societies not by a Balzacian cataloging of facts and events but by penetrating observations and often ironic contrasts. Julien Sorel's quest for happiness through love and power echoes ironically in Braz Cubas's materially comfortable but basically otiose life, while the calculating Fabrice of *La chartreuse de Parme* (1839) anticipates the kind of self-serving political and psychological insinuation so brilliantly depicted in *Epitaph of a Small Winner, Philosopher or Dog?*, and *Dom Casmurro*.

Flaubert, another writer surprisingly similar to Machado de Assis, was like his Brazilian counterpart an artist in whom romanticism and realism coexisted. And, like the Flaubert of *Madame Bovary* (1856), the Machado de Assis of 1880 and after was unwilling to create according to the dictates of the reading public. Both Flaubert and Machado broke radically with accepted literary conventions and strove to move their novels and stories into new and more valid realms of artistic expression. Machado, as much as Flaubert, sought *le mot juste,* the precise word or, in Machado's case, the precise image or metaphor to express the desired artistic end. This intense concern over careful language use led in both Flaubert and Machado to the development of singular styles that managed to be both poetically suggestive and full of nuance as well as referentially exact and concrete. In a way Emma Bovary's fatal predicament, that of being aware of a desire for romantic escapism and yet forced to live out the disappointing reality of her dreary everyday life, has a tragic parallel in the disastrous metamorphosis of the callow Bentinho (the narrator as a young man) into Dom Casmurro (the narrator as a reclusive and embittered old man). Machado and Flaubert also have similar styles in that each presents his characters indirectly, allowing them to build themselves detail by detail (with certain exceptions in the case of Machado) an absolute minimum of authorial intervention or explanation. Although

Machado, in the cases of Dom Casmurro or Braz Cubas, uses self-conscious but flawed narrator/protagonists, he achieves, largely through his use of both implied authors and implied readers, a kind of authorial objectivity that is both similar to, yet a departure from Flaubert's. Finally, both Flaubert and Machado make use of characters who possess ironic names and who objectify their own existences, separating themselves from their authors. Félicité ("happiness") of "Un coeur simple," for example, exemplifies a most unhappy life, while "Dom Casmurro" is a nickname the real meaning of which, if known to the reader of the novel entitled *Dom Casmurro,* would reveal a fatal defect in the personality of the character who calls himself "Dom Casmurro." Félicité, moreover, is a character who cannot be proven to represent the views of the man Flaubert, any more than the actions of the character Dom Casmurro need be taken as those of Machado de Assis. Though they achieve it in very different ways, both Flaubert and Machado de Assis give the novel form a new kind of objectivity, one in which the real author, to paraphrase Flaubert, is like God in the universe, "present everywhere" but "visible nowhere."

A writer often closely associated with Flaubert, and another writer with whom Machado de Assis has a great deal in common, is the American Henry James. James, who is often credited with being the father of the psychological novel, is like Machado less interested in the external world of action and event than in the inner lives of his characters, with the forces that drive them and lead them to make one decision rather than another. As Samuel Putnam, one of the first to point out the parallels between James and Machado, says, "Different as they are in many ways, Henry James and Machado de Assis have much in common. Both are novelists who deal in ideas; not ideas in the repellent abstract, but clothed in human form, made over into characters. Both are concerned with psychological analysis, with the nebulous action that takes place behind the curtained consciousness of men. If there is a difference between them it is largely one of depth. James, not too far beneath the surface, is apt to be content with the delicate shading, the subtle nuance that illuminates the fragile motivation of his figures as they move about in an atmosphere of aristocratic aloofness, while Machado de Assis goes on down to those forbidden regions of the soul where man may only venture at his peril."[9]

Both James and Machado like Flaubert before them share a deep commitment to the refinement of the novel as an art form, to the craft of fiction. While James and Machado apparently never knew of each other, they admired many of the same European masters. Machado, however, eventually rejecting French romanticism for the English tradition of Fielding, Swift,

Sterne, and others, gradually became both a more comic and a more philosophic novelist than James. Apropos of this Putnam notes that in his opinion James, for all his marvelous insight and subtlety, lacks Machado's "sabedoria," or profound life wisdom.[10] Both James and Machado are at their best when, as in *The Ambassadors* (1903) or *Dom Casmurro* (1900), they emphasize ironic structures, relationships, and interior characterization rather than external action. By focusing primarily on motives, circumstances, and the inner tumult that results from these, James and Machado each lead the novel toward a distinctly psychological orientation. Showing the reader why something happens rather than describing the event itself, they both work toward the establishment of what has come to be known as the psychological novel, a form in which characterization—one of Machado's strongest suits as a novelist—becomes especially important. Early in his career, however, in works like *Ressurreição* (1872), *Helena* (1876), and *Iaiá Garcia* (1878), Machado de Assis had begun in earnest to develop a technique that would show (and on occasion tell) how events or circumstances in the external, social world would produce often unexpected results in his character's minds, which are fraught psychologically with conflict, ambivalence, and inconsistency. Thus, one could reasonably argue that because he so early focused precisely on this kind of internalized drama, Machado de Assis, and not Henry James, deserves credit for having originated the modern psychological novel.

Novels like *Epitaph of a Small Winner, Dom Casmurro,* and *Philosopher or Dog?* and numerous of his post-1880 stories ("Midnight Mass" and "A Woman's Arms," for example) also recall Freud in the ways the conflicting forces of the unconscious, including those of a sexual nature, are portrayed and in the ways Machado like Freud shows how neurotic behavior can be a reflection of painful events or actions that have been repressed. A psychoanalytic interpretation of *Dom Casmurro* or *Philosopher or Dog?*, for example, would reveal—as Freud's own case histories do—that these texts, typical of modernist narrative, do not offer the reader stable, clear-cut, and logical conclusions about how reality is, but a flow of queries, hypotheses, and investigations that probe, often inconclusively, the tangled psychological web of human motivation and discourse. Both Freud and Machado describe men and women who, bedeviled from without by social circumstances and mores and from within by their own multifaceted and conflicting personalities, exist furtively in worlds they can neither explain nor control. One of Freud's therapies, that of conversational free association, in which his patients were encouraged to talk freely and to withhold, alter, or censor nothing, is strikingly similar to the form adopted by Machado in *Epitaph of a Small Winner* and

Dom Casmurro. If one imagines Braz Cubas, Dom Casmurro, and the narrator of "The Companion," for example, as the patients who are engaging in free association and the reader as the therapist who listens, the parallels between the nature of Freud's symbolically and metaphorically investigative case studies and Machado's ostensibly self-revelatory but in truth artfully ambiguous, acutely self-conscious, and self-serving narratives are clearly seen. Machado's masterpiece, *Dom Casmurro* (1900), and his atmospheric, marvelously vague, erotically charged, and dreamlike story, "Midnight Mass" (1894), both involve the kinds of psychoanalytic problems Freud was struggling with in his *Interpretation of Dreams* (1900) and in later works like *The Ego and the Id* (1923), which offered a further elaboration of Freud's division of the human mind's basic urges into the id, the ego, and the superego. Even Freud's work on the psychopathology of humor, *Jokes and their Relation to the Unconscious* (1905), can be illuminatingly applied to Machado's narratives and the unique kind of humor they present.

On the basis of what we know about Machado's intellectual prowess, his boundless curiosity, and his voracious reading habit, it is finally not out of the question to speculate that, since he had begun to study German as early as 1883, Machado might well have known about Freud and his work. Regardless of the possible influence of Freud on Machado, however, what is clear is that the Brazilian writer, like Fëdor Dostoyevski (with his similarly tragic vision of human life and his anguished, inward-looking, and existential narratives about characters painfully aware of their own, irreconcilable inner schisms), is an artist whose work uncannily anticipates the destructive psychological conflicts upon which Freud, only a few years later, cast so much light. A comparative consideration of Machado and Dostoyevski reveals that an interesting parallel can, for example, be drawn between the rationalistic nihilism of Ivan of *The Brothers Karamazov* (1880) and the elaborately disguised and comic but equally rationalized nihilism of Braz Cubas of *Epitaph of a Small Winner* (1880).[11]

A second Russian writer to whom Machado de Assis is closely akin is Chekhov, whose distinctly modernistic sense of life as being multilayered, controlled by unconscious urges as much as by conscious ones, and chiefly characterized by internalized conflicts, tensions, and self-deceptions, was largely shared by his Brazilian contemporary. Both Chekhov and Machado, moreover, give form to these typically unresolved conflicts and contradictions by means of a style meticulously designed not so much to describe, highlight, and put things into clear relief, as with the realists, but to suggest or imply the psychological complexity of their subjects and to deny the reader any facile explanations of the conflicts involved. Since both Chekhov and Machado develop characters who themselves do not fully understand the web of feelings and thoughts that envelops them, they do not make use of a style that explicates and communicates directly and unambiguously to the reader. Rather, Chekhov like Machado draws the reader into an active if uncertain participation in the story, which changes in accordance with the reader's evolving interpretation of the conflict. As evidenced in works like *The Cherry Orchard* (1904), "Ward Number Six" (1892), "About Love" (1898; love also being one of Machado's prime concerns), and "Gooseberries" (1898), Chekhov, like the Machado of *Epitaph of a Small Winner* "The Psychiatrist," "Midnight Mass," *Philosopher or Dog?*, and *Dom Casmurro,* develops a richly ironic technique, one in which what appears to be true very often is not. Although Chekhov's often disoriented characters are typically portrayed in the context of a society that is disintegrating (czarist Russia of the 1860s and 1870s), Machado's most memorable characters are typically the complacently self-satisfied, upper middle-class members of a very stable and smugly secure social world, that of Brazil's Second Empire (1840–90). Internally, however, the characters of both writers anticipate the sterility, disillusionment, and nihilism of the modernists, whose splintered and angst-ridden world Eliot, for example, described in *The Waste Land* (1922).

Though Chekhov is on balance less despairing than Machado in his view of life, both writers possess a sardonically comic sense of human existence. In "Ward Number Six," for example, Chekhov relates the story of a doctor who, failing to take proper care of the patients in a mental hospital, is himself eventually committed to it. This story has an interesting counterpart in Machado's "Psychiatrist" (1882), a similarly ironic tale in which another doctor, blinded by what he unquestioningly takes to be the flawlessly curative powers of science, ends up committing himself to a hospital for the insane. "Gooseberries," on the other hand, a Chekhov story that, like many of Machado's, seems on one level to be without either action, plot, or resolution, gradually reveals itself to be about the human problems of self-delusion, emotional paralysis, and spiritual crisis, themes that are endemic to Machado's mature fiction. Machado's most compelling characters, like those of Chekhov, fall prey to self-induced and self-deluding retreats from life. But while Chekhov's people often find solace in love and honest labor, Machado's, awash in a sea of modernist ennui, typically fail to find any salvation. Like Eliot's "hollow men," Machado's characters are materially well-off but spiritually and morally bankrupt, either unable or, worse, unwilling to do what is necessary to give meaning and dignity to their lives.

Finally, there is the case of de Maupassant, another major narrativist of the nineteenth century with whom Machado can be revealingly compared. Like de Maupassant, Machado is at his most trenchant when writing about average middle-class men and women. Also like de Maupassant, Machado did much of his finest work in the short story genre, a form that both writers control brilliantly to show the cupidity, savagery, and selfishness that lie hidden behind the hypocritical facade of bourgeois respectability and morality. Neither writer typically makes any explicit moral judgement about his characters but instead works indirectly, leading the reader to determine the morality of the semantically ambiguous messages that arise from the characters' conduct and words. Portrayed as being midway between the idealized innocent of the romantics and the animalistic brutes of the naturalists, the characters created by Machado and de Maupassant are, as described by both Pascal and Machado, caught between brutality and angelicism, between "l'ange et la bête" (Assis, *Epitaph,* 80). Yet because they are, especially in Machado's case, ambivalently attracted to both these poles, these characters are paralyzed, mired in their comfortable material affluence and often simply uninterested in developing in any direction. The result, laconically depicted by both Machado and de Maupassant, is the sense of stasis so characteristic of modernist literature. A preoccupation in their greatest works with showing how the hypocritical attitudes of their characters reflect the debased moral standards of a certain segment of society is one reason both de Maupassant and Machado de Assis are often described as pessimists as well as realists. Several of de Maupassant's stories, "Boule de suif" (1880), "La maison Tellies" (1881), and "Mademoiselle Fifi" (1883), for example, have parallels in many of Machado's post-1880 stories, few of which can be said to offer an overtly optimistic view of human conduct.

The gradual "discovery" of Machado in the second half of the twentieth century has raised the question of how he should be read. Should Machado de Assis be interpreted essentially as a realist or, as many critics maintain, a modernist?[12] The former group, represented by John Gledson in *The Deceptive Realism of Machado de Assis,* views Machado's "realism" prescriptively, as ideology rather than as literary style, and thus places Machado's texts in a distinctly historical or sociopolitical perspective.[13] But unlike such rote realists as William Dean Howells and George Eliot, who espouse a basically mimetic and pragmatic theory of art, Machado, with his emphasis on interiorized conflict, symbolically rendered characterizations, and controlled ambiguity, created a body of literature the theoretical or aesthetic base of which, especially after 1880, can be described as largely, if not essentially, impressionistic and even modernistic. In Machado's day impressionism was a type of literary criticism favored by Anatole France, one of the first non-Brazilian authorities to recognize (in his 3 April 1909 speech at the Sorbonne on "Le Génie Latin) Machado's brilliance. As a critic France might well have had Machado's work in mind when he described impressionistic criticism as "the adventures of a sensitive soul among masterpieces." Yet for all this, Machado's sense of what criticism and the critic should do shows him to be closer to Charles-Augustin Sainte-Beuve than to France.

But for all Machado's realistic tendencies, it seems only partially accurate to place him in the context of such prototypically realistic writers as Fielding, Jane Austen, George Eliot, Balzac, and Dickens. As with other great writers, Machado's work defies any kind of narrow categorization. Like James Joyce, Machado weaves a sharply rendered realism with a powerfully unifying symbolism to produce works of literature that, though based on accurate descriptions of a particular place and time, also generate universal statements about the human condition. The social and geographic details presented in "Araby," "The Dead," or *Ulysses,* for example, like those presented in "Midnight Mass," "Mariana," and *Dom Casmurro,* amount to a literary portrait that realistically reproduces a certain place (Dublin and Rio de Janeiro) while at the same time making comments that symbolically are germane to men and women everywhere. Like Joyce Machado merges the modes of realism with those of symbolism in the creation of a new literary language, one characterized by both metonymy and, especially, metaphor.

Although we can agree that Machado de Assis unquestionably makes use of certain realistic themes, motifs, and techniques, it is also clear that on balance he exhibits many if not all of the themes, motifs, and techniques of literary modernism. Some of Machado's more conspicuous modernistic tendencies include the following: narratives often metafictionally self-conscious about their own form and "truthfulness"; narratives that concentrate not on external action but on the presentation of inner states of consciousness; narratives that elicit in the reader a sense of the nihilism, philistinism, and randomness that lie behind the ordered (that is, realistically portrayed) surface appearance of life and reality; narratives that challenge the legitimacy of bourgeois morality and ethics; and narratives that are formally inventive, that flout rigid conventions about what "reality" is and how it can best be reproduced, challenging the need for linear, cause-and-effect related plot structures.[14]

In his themes, too, Machado shows himself to be essentially modernistic. By emphasizing such modernist staples as the sense, pervasive in his work, that in Brazil, as in human affairs generally, "Things fall apart; the center cannot hold" (W. B. Yeats, "The Second Coming"); that time corrodes and eventually destroys everything; that, painfully conscious of our duplicity and temporality, we human beings are confused about how we should live, about the choices we must make; that we are forced to live in a universe utterly indifferent to our fate; and that appearances are always deceiving, Machado proves himself to be an early protomodernist.

Although they come and go in a realistically recreated social milieu, Machado's characters, like Eliot's, Joyce's, Albert Camus's, or Mann's, are very much alone. Struggling with their own inner demons, which are both exacerbated and mollified by changing social circumstances, the men and women of Machado's bleak fictive world often express what would later be described as an existential sense of existence, one summed up in the final lines of *Philosopher or Dog?*: "If you have tears, weep for these two not long dead. But if you have only laughter, laugh. It is all the same. The Southern Cross, . . . is too high in the heavens to distinguish between man's laughter and tears."[15] Reminiscent of Eliot in his ironic use of myth (*Esau and Jacob* and *Counselor Ayres' Memorial* are notably "mythic" novels), of Proust in his handling of time and memory,[16] of Joyce in his metafictionally comedic yet philosophically serious sense of life, and of Mann in his vision of the crucial yet puzzling roles art and the artist play in modern life, Machado de Assis anticipated in the years between 1880 and 1908 many of the forms, themes, and techniques associated with European modernism. Although, as Roberto Schwarz, Gledson, and others maintain, Machado can indeed be classified as a realist, he is less like such orthodox realists as Balzac, Dickens, or Turgenev than he is like such modernistically hybrid writers as James, Hardy, Chekhov, de Maupassant, Proust, or Joyce, artists who combine psychological portraiture with the techniques of both realism and symbolism to forge a new literature for a new age.

In our now slightly expanded history of the Western novel, then, we can see how Machado de Assis provides the crucial missing link between the realism of Flaubert's *Madame Bovary* and the modernism of Joyce's *Ulysses*. Closer on balance to the latter than to the former, works like *Epitaph of a Small Winner, Philosopher or Dog?, Páginas recolhidas, Dom Casmurro, Esau and Jacob,* and *Counselor Ayres' Memorial* prove that Machado de Assis deserves recognition not merely as Brazil's first great narrativist but as one of the true masters of modern narrative in the Western tradition.

Chapter Three
The Major Themes

A thematic approach to the fiction, poetry, and dramatic literature of Machado de Assis reveals an artist who reproduces a certain social and political milieu, who compels the reader to contemplate his or her own specific condition, and who leads us to contemplate the nature of human existence in general. Like all great writers, Machado creates fictive worlds populated by characters whose private hopes, fears, and struggles are projected onto a universal plane. Thus it is that characters such as "Dom Casmurro," Capitú or Braz Cubas, like Don Quixote, Werther, or Emma Bovary, come to life in the context of a specific work of art at the same time that they gain an existence beyond it, expressing some quality or dimension of the human condition that all people everywhere can appreciate. Whether perceived as a realist or a modernist, Machado is unquestionably a novelist of ideas, a deeply philosophic writer whose major themes involve some of humanity's most fundamental concerns. In short, Machado de Assis is the kind of writer whose art, as Everett W. Knight says, "expresses the truth, the nature of which is to be ambiguous."[1]

Although the great majority of Machado's primary themes deal with the eternal questions of human existence, he was also concerned with the nature and function of time in human affairs as well as with issues of a more directly sociopolitical relevance. For purposes of comparative analysis, however, it is useful to divide Machado's basic themes into the following categories: metaphysical concerns, especially the conflict between love (of others) and love of one's self (egoism); the destructive effects of time; the isolation and progressive disillusionment of each human being; a sense of human existence as being at once tragic and absurd; and, finally, the need for individual action, choice, and strength of will. Because Machado's basic themes, often with fascinating variations, are reiterated throughout his work, as Afrânio Coutinho remarks, they offer the reader an unusually useful insight into not only the nature of particular texts themselves but into Machado's own aesthetic consciousness as well. While one can easily agree with Coutinho that the bulk of Machado's thematic concerns fall into the category of metaphysical speculation about life, death, and the contradictory nature of human existence,[2] it is revealing of Machado's great range as a writer to subdivide this capacious category into smaller, more sharply focused groups.

Arguably the Ur-theme of Machado's work, the problem of love in human existence is endemic to his writings. When cast in the perspective of his metaphysical concerns about life, one can see that the question of love for Machado de Assis involved an ontological problem of the highest order: does one love one's self or does one love someone else? Integrally connected to the closely related issue of human motivation, the problem of love in human affairs led Machado to ask, in a number of different novels, plays, stories, and poems, what motivates people, what leads them to act one way and not another? Identifying unrestrained egoism, or self-interest, as the most insidious of human urges, and showing it as being constantly at odds with our nobler urges, such as love of others and magnanimity, Machado created a variety of works in which questions of moral or ethical choice are centrally involved. Because in the main Machado's characters choose to let self-interest guide their actions and choices—even when it results directly or indirectly in the exploitation, injury, or slighting of someone else—critics have long judged Machado to be a pessimistic writer, one whose own supposed disillusionment with life infuses his work with an air of bitter resignation. To what extent this view is valid cannot be accurately determined and Machado himself stated more than once that his works were not to be interpreted in terms of his life. Nevertheless, it seems also very likely that at least some of the stringently pessimistic weltanschauung that permeates novels like *Epitaph of a Small Winner, Philosopher or Dog?,* and *Dom Casmurro,* stories like "The Bonzo's Secret," "Wallow, Swine," "Alexandrian Tale," and "The Companion," and poems like "A causa secreta" (The secret cause), "The Blue Fly," and "Suave mari magno" is an expression of how Machado felt about life. But at the same time running through all these darkly negative works is the idea that our lives do not have to be this way, that by making different choices we could create more satisfying existences for ourselves. It is in this ethical context that we see the force of love playing so decisive a thematic role in Machado's work.

In the early narratives, dramas, and poems, Machado developed the theme of love in a more or less conventional fashion, one generally consistent with the established tenets of French romanticism that were then guiding him. The well-written but basically undistinguished stories of such early collections as *Contos fluminenses* (1869) and *Histórias da meia-noite* (1873) are, like the poems and novels of Machado's pre-1880 period, largely jejune love stories and parlor intrigues that, if taken as a whole, constitute, "a mildly ironic but pleasant and entertaining portrait of a miniature Belle Epoque in a Brazilian setting."[3] As early as Machado's first novel, *Ressurreição* (1872), however, the theme of love, central to the novel's plot, is developed as involving the consequences of a life lived by loving another human being versus one lived by loving one's self. Felix, the semitragic protagonist, allows his selfishness, his self-doubt, and his jealousy to destroy his love for Livia, the heroine, who, responding to his love, could have saved, or "resurrected," him from his own worst impulses, from his pernicious egoism.

Although this same theme is played out in a more complex fashion, and with considerable variation, in the other novels of Machado's "romantic" phase, *The Hand and the Glove* (1874), *Helena* (1876), and *Iaiá Garcia* (1878), it gets a new and powerful treatment in *Epitaph of a Small Winner* (1880), the first novel of Machado's "realistic" or "mature" phase and one of his greatest achievements. In this landmark work, which recalls Dickens's *Posthumous Papers of the Pickwick Club*,[4] the character Braz Cubas shows the reader what an existence based purely on egoism would be like. Always concerned with the illusory nature of things, with the question of appearance versus truth, Machado suggests that while Braz's well-heeled life appears to be laudable and satisfying, it is in truth the cold, barren, and utterly selfish life of a materially comfortable but spiritually bankrupt nihilist. The outwardly affable Braz Cubas is the prototype of the Machadoan character who loves himself more than anything or anyone else. The text subtly establishes the primacy of Braz's egoism early on in a hallucinatory chapter that has him absurdly astride a hippopotamus flying backwards through time. Encountering a strange female figure, Braz asks who and what she is. The figure answers that she is Nature, or Pandora, and, paradoxically, that she is both Braz's mother and his enemy. Seeing that this revelation alarms Braz, Nature then says, "Do not be afraid. . . ." "[M]y enmity does not kill; it is through life that it affirms itself. You are alive: I wish you no other calamity" (31). By suggesting here in a comic mode that the "enmity" of "Nature" is thus affirmed through "life" itself, and that humanity and nature have a distinctly ambivalent relationship (Nature being both Braz's "mother" and his "enemy"), Machado posits a view of human existence that anticipates the twentieth-century philosophy of existentialism. When an increasingly credulous Braz asks Nature, moreover, "Was it not you who gave me life and placed in my heart the love of life? Then why should you do yourself injury by killing me?" Machado is allowing one of his most famous and fascinating characters to enunciate a question that has long daunted philosophers, artists, and theologians: why is death the end result of life?

Then, in a scene that brilliantly entwines Machado's metaphysical concerns about the transitory nature of human existence, the ravages wrought by

time, and the perverting presence of egoism, Nature answers Braz's query
by saying:

Because I have no more need of you. Time finds interest not in the minute that is already passing, but only in the minute that is about to come. The new-born minute is
strong, merry, thinks that it carries eternity in its bosom; it brings only death, and
perishes like its predecessors. But I do not perish. Egoism, you say? Yes, egoism; I
have no other law. Egoism, self-preservation. The tiger kills the lamb because the tiger's philosophy is that, above all, it must live, and if the lamb is tender so much the
better; this is the universal law.

(33)

When Braz with no difficulty at all accepts Nature's assertion that egoism is
the "universal law" of existence, he makes manifest a philosophical position
about how he has lived his life that allows him to be comfortable with the
utter indifference he has shown throughout his existence to the fate of others.
This integral theme is replayed in Machado's masterpiece, *Dom Casmurro,*
where it is not just egoism but egoism coupled with jealousy, working in consort with the corrosion of love and the passage of time, that conspire to destroy the protagonist.

Although *Epitaph of a Small Winner* may well constitute the prototypical
expression of the theme of love of others versus love of self, or egoism, in
Machado's work, it appears elsewhere as well, in poems like "A partida" (The
parting,) "Erro" (Error), and "Uma oda de Anacreonte," and in the late play
"Lição de botânica." The novel *Philosopher or Dog?,* too, shows selfishness to
be the basic motivating force for virtually everyone in the novel; of the major
characters, only the insane protagonist, Rubião, whose love for the vain and
sensuous Sofia is first manipulated and then spurned, escapes its fatal lure,
and then only by "virtue" of madness.

One of the lesser-noticed aspects of this theme is the role sensuousness
plays in it. In the stories "Midnight Mass," "A Strange Thing," and "A Woman's Arms," and in poems like "Cognac" and "Sofá," a powerful though
muted erotic charge animates the text. In "Midnight Mass," for example,
widely held to be one of Machado's most finely crafted stories, the female
protagonist, Conceição, is made to seem as if, perhaps unconsciously, she is
flirting with the young male narrator or—and again it is marvelously
uncertain—actually trying in a desultory fashion to entice him into some
kind of sexual encounter. The story, a model of artfully poised ambiguity, reminds one of the treatment love receives in Joyce's "The Dead," a story
where, as in "Midnight Mass," love is shown erotically and idealistically to

have both a unifying and a divisive presence in human affairs. In "A Woman's Arms," however, the sensual dimension of love, which is more explicitly developed than in "Midnight Mass," is powerfully linked to the basic self-centeredness of each character, a facet of its presentation that connects it to several of Machado's other well-known narratives including "The Secret Heart," "The Rod of Justice," "Father versus Mother," "The Admiral's Night," and "The Education of a Stuffed Shirt." The latter work, with its open advocacy of hypocrisy as the proper, most "rewarding" approach to life, recalls C. S. Lewis's *Screwtape Papers,*[5] a story that, like several of Machado's stories and novels, ties both hypocrisy and a shallow materialism to an essentially egotistical approach to life.

Of Machado's later works, his final novel, *Counselor Ayres' Memorial,* is unique in that being a celebration of both life and love (of another person) it shows the powerfully unified existence that can result when people consciously and unstintingly put the happiness and welfare of their mate ahead of their own. If *Epitaph of a Small Winner* shows the defeat of love by egoism, then *Counselor Ayres' Memorial* depicts the ennobling victory of love over the debasing but ever seductive forces of egoism and selfishness.

So frequently do expressions of the corrosive effects of time appear in Machado's work that this theme, too, may be considered one of his most definitive concerns. Pre-Proustian in its melancholy significance for writers of the early twentieth century, this theme, along with its modernist corollary, that only art can withstand the destruction wrought by the passage of time, also permeates Machado's writings. It stands at the core of novels like *Dom Casmurro, Epitaph of a Small Winner,* and *Philosopher or Dog?,* of stories like "The Looking Glass," "Final Request," "Viver!" (Life), "Dona Paula," "Eternal," and "Mariana," and of numerous poems, including "O desfecho" (The outcome), "Sonêto de Natal" (Christmas sonnet), "Minha musa" (My muse), "O profeta" (The prophet), "A um poeta" (To a poet), "A missão do poeta" (The mission of the poet), "Musa consolatrix" (Consoling muse), and "No alto" (On high).

"Sonêto de Natal" (1896) and *Dom Casmurro,* for example, develop as their themes "the impossibility of reconstructing the past" while "O desfecho" and the 1886 story "Life" deal not only with the relentless flow of time but with the resignation or *tedium vitae* that a realization of this truth can effect in human beings.[6] In the earlier sonnet, an ironic metapoem similar in this respect to the often ironically metafictional post-1880 narratives, we learn of a man who tried unsuccessfully first to remember and then to commit to verse the days of his childhood and the sensations of youth and innocence that accompanied them. Failing to achieve this comforting end, the voice resignedly concludes by asking, "Was it Christmas that changed, or was it me?"[7]

In *Dom Casmurro* the narrator, like the voice in the sonnet, wants to go back to an earlier time. Explaining to the reader his motives for building in his old age a house that meticulously reproduces the house he lived in as a child he says, "My purpose was to tie together the two ends of my life, to restore adolescence in old age."[8] But, as in the case of "Sonêto de Natal," the narrator sadly discovers that he cannot connect his present with his long gone past. The final, self-conscious line of the sonnet—"Was it Christmas that changed, or was it me?"—presages a similar yet more complex and duplicitously evasive thought in *Dom Casmurro:* "Well, sir, I did not succeed in putting back together what had been nor what I had been. . . . A man consoles himself more or less for those he has lost, but I myself am missing, and this lack is essential" (5).

A variation on this same fundamental theme appears in the short story "Mariana," which, as Lorie Ishimatsu points out, is the narrative counterpart of the poem "Sabina," one of the less distinguished poetic compositions in *Americanas*.[9] In "Mariana," however, a story first published in 1871, Machado concerns himself with the differences between psychological and chronological time and with the uncertain relationship between life and art. Speaking of one of the main characters, whose point of view dominates the story's telling, the narrative voice declares, "time had passed in a peculiar manner: although to Evaristo it seemed that three hours had gone by, everything had actually happened within five or six minutes. . . ."[10] Later, this same character discovers that "she did not descend from the canvas as the Mariana of his imagination had done, but from time. . . . [A]nd as he recalled the portrait in the salon, Evaristo concluded that art was superior to nature—the canvas had retained the body and the soul" (122).

Closely allied to the theme of time's destructive and inexorable passing is another of Machado's primary concerns, that of the illusory nature of things, the discrepancy between appearance and reality, and the sense of disillusionment and isolation that stems from our discovery that things are seldom what they seem. To the extent that we are justified in speaking of an author's personal world view and its relation to his or her art, we would be hard pressed to disagree with the majority of critics who hold that Machado's sense of human reality is one in which there is a constant clash of antithetical forces, social as well as psychological, and that in nearly all cases evil, or its numerous analogues, such as egoism, jealousy, pretentiousness, cowardice, and lethargy, win out. Though Machado's work is regularly written in a droll style that contains a great deal of ironic and incisive humor, the fictive worlds he builds are anything but funny. In reading Machado's work, especially his post-1880 fiction and poetry, one is struck time and time again by the oddly unsettling sensation of laughing about things that are on sober reconsideration essentially tragic. To understand this discrepancy, which occurs more often on the part of the reader (who must live with its full human significance) than the characters (who seldom realize it), is to be able to account for the profound sense of ontological seriousness that underlies all of Machado's outwardly wry texts.

Outstanding not only in terms of the sheer number of titles that fall within it, this thematic category also includes some of Machado's finest efforts, in narrative as well as poetry and drama. Of the novels that deal with these themes, *Epitaph of a Small Winner, Philosopher or Dog?, Esau and Jacob,* and *Dom Casmurro* stand out. In his short fiction, one would call attention to such exemplary stories as "The Devil's Church," "Final Request," "The Psychiatrist," "Alexandrian Tale," "Adam and Eve," and "The Companion." Of Machado's poetic expression of the intertwined themes of isolation and disillusionment, of appearance versus reality and of the illusory nature of things, several works deserve special mention: "Mundo interior" (Interior world), "Uma criatura" (A creature), "Potira" (Potira), "A môsca azul" ("The Blue Fly"), "Ultima jornada" (Final Journey), "A partida" (The parting), and "Círculo vicioso" ("Vicious Circle"). In drama, *Quase ministro* treats this theme, as does *Lição de botânica.*

Of all his works that deal with the illusory (and beguiling) aspects of life, few sum up this essential Machadoan theme as succinctly as "A môsca azul" ("The Blue Fly"), a poem said by Isaac Goldberg to be "almost an epitome of [Machado's] outlook, revealing as it does his tender irony, his human pity, his repressed sensuality, his feeling for form, his disillusioned comprehension of illusions."[11] In this key poem it is, ironically enough, a "beautiful" blue fly that so entrances a humble man. Increasingly mesmerized by the fly's radiant appearance (that is, by life), he attempts to seize it (experience life and explain it rationally) in order to examine it more closely and thereby understand it better. In doing so, the man ironically destroys the very thing that has so attracted him. Now tormented because he knows neither how nor why he caused its destruction, the man goes mad, never understanding how he lost his beautiful blue fly, that is, life itself.

In response to the man who has asked the fly from whence it received its "glitter," its appeal, the insect, already an ironic symbol of the beauties of human existence, self-consciously extends itself into a larger, more ontological metaphor by saying, "I am life." It thus reiterates essentially what Nature (Pandora) had said to Braz Cubas in *Epitaph of a Small Winner.* Moreover, the swoonlike trance that the blue fly's glitter effects on the man in the poem is very similar to Braz's delirium. And when the man in "The Blue Fly," overcome by the fly's external appearance and thinking himself somehow equal to it, envisions himself a king, he echoes the pathetic Rubião of *Philosopher or Dog?,* a character whose only satisfaction in life had been achieved in a state of insanity, when he, too, imagined himself to be a king. "To the victor, the potatoes!" Rubião shouted to the curious idlers. "Here I am Emperor! . . . A few days later he died. . . . Before the onset of his agony, which was short, he placed the crown upon his head . . . he alone saw the imperial insignia . . ." (270–71).

Dealing with a closely related theme, that of our gnawing incapacity to be content with what we have, Machado's famous sonnet, "Círculo vicioso," has also established itself as one of his most telling statements concerning the dissatisfied nature of human existence. Cogently expressed in "Círculo vicioso," this sense of bitterness, weariness, and disillusionment—of *tedium vitae*—permeates Machado's work, but it is especially apparent (as in the story "Life") in his post-1880 poetry, prose, and theater. Apropos of this issue, Goldberg and others have thought, indeed, that in the final lines of Machado's poetic tribute to Artur de Oliveira, a fellow Brazilian poet saluted in *Ocidentais,* he is really writing about himself: "You will laugh, not with the ancient laughter, long and powerful,—the laughter of an eternal friendly youth, but with another, a bitter laughter, like the laughter of an ailing god, who wearies of divinity and who, too, longs for an end. . . ."[12]

Nietzschean not in the sense of advocating any kind of "will to power" superman ethic but in the determination to offer both an honest artistic and intellectual interpretation of human existence and a profound objection to the hypocrisy, crassness, and complacency of Brazil's Second Empire bourgeoisie, this poem and other works like it show Machado de Assis to be a truly universal writer, whose essentially philosophic outlook did not prevent him, as it did not prevent Nietzsche, from being a penetrating cultural critic of his age. Both Machado and Nietzsche—the one in fiction, the other in philosophy—presage the angst, disillusionment, and estrangement that characterize the modernist period. It may be of interest to note finally in terms of other possible parallels between Nietzsche and Machado, that both were profoundly influenced by the "pessimistic" and ironic philosophy of Arthur Schopenhauer (1788–1860).[13]

In some ways an extension of the sense of disillusionment that accompanies a realization of the illusory nature of reality, the themes of pessimism and nihilism also constitute a major category of Machado's work. Although these themes have traditionally been said to characterize the outlook of Machado de Assis himself, there is no verifiable biographical evidence that he ever conducted himself and his affairs in accordance with these intensely negative attitudes.

Yet if Machado himself lived an exemplary life—one characterized by personal and professional generosity, by sensitivity and commitment to his wife, Dona Carolina, and by an unswerving dedication to his art—his texts, and especially his late fiction and poetry, have led generations of readers to conclude that this great Brazilian writer, a politically progressive patriot as well as a gregarious person and respected artist, was really a bitter misanthrope possessed of an intensely negative view of the human condition. It is, indeed, largely from this striking contrast between the life lived by the man and the view of life depicted, especially in his post-1880 works, that, in conjunction with his refusal to discuss his works, the enigmatic mystery surrounding Machado de Assis has evolved. We know that Machado wanted people to interpret his books without making reference to the events and circumstances of his life,[14] but we also realize upon reading his later novels, stories, poems, and dramatic works that Machado could generate a picture of life that, if not despairing, was at least deeply skeptical about the moral and ethical conduct of most men and women, about the likelihood that in any given circumstance we will do what is generous, supportive, or good rather than what is narrow, selfish, and evil.

In novels like *Epitaph of a Small Winner, Philosopher or Dog?,* and *Dom Casmurro,* in stores like "Alexandrine Tale," "The Secret Heart," "Life," "The Devil's Church," "The Education of a Stuffed Shirt," "The Bonzo's Secret," "The Companion," "The Diplomat," and "Wallow, Swine!" and in poems like "Aspiração" (Aspiration), "No limiar" (On the threshold), "No alto" (On high), "Un vieux pays" (An old country), "O desfecho" (The outcome), "Suave mari magno," "Uma criatura" (A creature), "Niâni" (Niani), and "Perguntas sem resposta" (Answerless questions), Machado deftly but relentlessly paints a picture of the world that is dismally pessimistic, one in which nihilism, or a nihilistic sense of life, begins to seem the only naturally occurring and therefore legitimate approach to living. This sense of nihilism is the inner demon of Machado's work, as it is for such other modernist masters as Yeats, Joyce, Eliot, Luigi Pirandello, Franz Kafka, and Mann,[15] and it is his handling of it, coupled with the Nietzschean antibourgeois sentiment that animates it, that makes his post-1880 work so powerfully modernistic. In *Epitaph of a Small Winner,* for example, the essential nihilism of the main character, Braz Cubas, is an eventual outgrowth of the cynicism that, in a direct address to the reader, he says he does not have, but which, as the actively involved and attentive reader (the kind of reader Machado wanted to have) comes to realize, he does have. As Braz, ever the affable if duplicitous narrator, says, in a calculated attempt to disavow the label of cynic (which his actions if not his words prove he deserves), "To a Sensitive Soul: Among the five or ten readers of this book, there is a sensitive soul who is irritated with me because of the preceding chapter, is beginning to tremble for Eugenia's fate, and perhaps . . . yes, perhaps, in his heart, is calling me a cynic. I, a cynic, sensitive soul? By Diana's thigh! . . . Such an insult would have to be washed away with blood, if blood ever washed away anything in this world. No, sensitive soul, I was no cynic, I was merely a man . . . (91). As the careful reader perceives, however, Braz's selfishly callous treatment of the lame girl Eugenia does in fact reflect a deeply rooted cynicism on his part in spite of what he says. Indeed, it is Braz's unwitting revelation of his own gradual degeneration from selfishness to cynicism to nihilism that gives his narrative its comic yet chilling appeal. Braz's nihilism becomes apparent only in the final scene, when, ever the moral relativist, he is taking stock of his life (from the fixed perspective of the after life): "Adding up and balancing all these items, a person will conclude that my accounts showed neither a surplus nor a deficit and consequently that I died quits with life. And he will conclude falsely; for, upon arriving on this other side of the mystery, I found that I had a small surplus, which provides the final negative of this chapter of negatives: I have no progeny, I transmitted to no one the legacy of our misery" (250–51). Ironically expressed, Braz's final "surplus," in which he takes inordinate pleasure, is inherently nihilistic because it spells the end of the human race. By identifying "misery" with human existence, and by taking pride in having helped bring no children into the world, Braz is affirming the extinction of the species. His is a stark though complete affirmation of nihilism, an approach to life in which nothing, not even the engendering of children, has value.

With only a few exceptions an overwhelmingly pessimistic world view dominates the poetry, prose, and drama of Machado's post-1880 period. In "Suave mari magno" and "The Secret Heart," for example, Machado develops the concept that we humans take pleasure in observing the suffering of others. While the sonnet, described by Ishimatsu as "one of Machado's bleakest commentaries on human nature,"[16] remains relatively benign in telling how passers-by delight in observing the death throes of a dog, the 1885 short story develops an even crueler thought. Expanding upon the theme passively taken up in the poem, the narrative comes to suggest rather graphically that not only do we enjoy seeing other creatures suffer, we enjoy causing them to suffer: "And with a strange smile, reflection of a soul replete with satisfaction, a smile that told of an inward savoring of the most exquisite sensation, Fortunato cut off the rat's third paw, and for the third time made the same movement into the flame. The wretched animal squealed and twisted its bloodied, singed body, and would not die. . . . Garcia . . . looked intently at Fortunato's face. Neither rage nor hate; only a vast pleasure, quiet and deep, . . ."[17] The distinctive moral ambiguity of these later works is, as Meyer and others have shown,[18] a consciously rendered artistic vision of what Machado took the essential nature of human reality to be, that is, post-structurally relativistic and unstable, in which such concepts as truth and falsity, goodness and evil, or morality and immorality are often one and the same, a function of such variables as time, circumstance, and perspective.

Yet if poems like "No alto" (the final poem of *Ocidentais*), "Suave mari magno," and "Uma criatura," stories like "The Secret Heart" and "The Devil's Church," and novels like *Epitaph of a Small Winner* and *Philosopher or Dog?* all evoke an absurd, pessimistic, and even despairing sense of the human experience, certain others of Machado's works suggest another attitude, one if not exactly optimistic then at least potentially more ennobling. More stoic than nihilistic, this alternative to the otherwise bleak human and natural landscape painted by Machado's later works appears only occasionally, and then nearly always through a minor character, whose existence, often overlooked, acts as a foil to the other, more typically egoistic Machadoan characters. For example, figures like Dona Fernanda of *Philosopher or Dog?* and Eugenia and Dona Placida of *Epitaph of a Small Winner* struggle to maintain some shred of human dignity in an exploitive and compassionless world. Braz shows the depths of his mean-spirited hypocrisy by taking advantage of Dona Placida's penury to drag her into the morass of his own moral corruption and, because she is lame, he rejects the love of the other otherwise beautiful Eugenia, a casually cruel act of disregard that highlights yet another dimension of his superficial and self-centered existence. Yet in spite of being lame, rejected in love, and of very modest means, it is Eugenia, through her stoic refusal to acquiesce to the moral degeneration that her humble lot in life seems to demand of her, who exhibits dignified human conduct. There is a nobility to Eugenia that derives from her struggle to sustain a modicum of simple human decency for herself, a dignity that Braz, for all his wealth, good looks, and social station, has long since lost. The need for perseverance and endurance in life is shown in *Epitaph of a Small Winner* not only in Eugenia, however, but through the words of Quincas Borba, the "mad" philosopher. Scolding Braz Cubas for letting himself "slide down the fatal slope of melancholy," Quincas tells his friend: "My dear Braz Cubas, don't let yourself suffer from these old-fashioned vapors. What the devil, you have to be a man! Be strong! Fight! Conquer! Shine! Influence! Dominate!

. . . Courage Braz Cubas; . . . Why should you be bothered by the fact that everything moves along?" (224). Following hard on these artfully ambiguous admonitions, which in the context of the novel, the alert reader can interpret as either the babble of a raving lunatic or the sound advice of a man who, recognizing the chaos of a universe entirely indifferent to his welfare, consciously commits himself to be his own man, to take charge of his life, to be what he wishes to be, Quincas goes on to say, "You'll fight. Maybe you'll smash them and maybe you won't; the main thing is to fight. Life is struggle. A life without fighting is a dead sea in the universal organism" (230). Read narrowly as the wild ramblings of a madman, Quincas's words make little sense, especially for the morally phlegmatic Braz. But read in a wider context, that of an existentialist view of life, the reader can legitimately feel that even in his "madness" Quincas Borba is right; life is a struggle (as Machado repeatedly shows), and we humans must constantly make the moral and ethical choices that give meaning to our lives and that define us. Eugenia and Quincas would have understood what Jean-Paul Sartre meant when he said that existence precedes essence.

This same potentially ennobling existentialist sentiment can be found in such pre-1880 novels as *The Hand and the Glove* and *Iaiá Garcia* but it plays a major role in Machado's later works, including his last novel, *Counselor Ayres' Memorial,* where, bound up with the theme of love for others, it constitutes the text's thematic core. In theoretical terms Machado suggests in these works that although we may live in an absurd and contradictory universe, we as individuals can still exercise our willpower and self-control. We are, as Sören Kierkegaard (a theologian Machado might have admired), Nietzsche, Sartre, and Camus maintained, free to choose; indeed, as Machado might have put it, we are condemned to choose. One feels then that the one possibly redeeming feature of human existence that, though generally buried under a blanket of pessimism and gloom, occasionally makes its presence felt in Machado's fictional world is that envisaged by the existentialists, who held views similar to Machado's about human fate and the anguished nature of our painfully self-conscious existence in an indifferent and absurd universe.

Although critics continue to categorize Machado de Assis as a pessimistic writer, there is more to it than this. Indeed, Machado himself, as Caldwell notes, objected to being labeled a pessimist or skeptic ("céptico"), if used as a term of opprobrium, arguing that for him an optimist was simply an idiot but a pessimist was an idealist.[19] Thus, as critics like Caldwell, Maria Luisa Nunes, Albert Bagby, Jr., and others have suggested, one may fairly consider Machado himself to have been less a pessimist in the negative sense of the term than a realist, that is, one who simply describes life as it is and who lives as best he can. Bagby, for example, says of two important early novels, *Iaiá Garcia* and *The Hand and the Glove,* that "despite nature's indifference to man's strivings in Assis's world, these two novels do offer the insightful reader examples of man's triumph over adversity, and his consequent happiness as a result of his determination and strength. If some would not call this optimism, it is at least not pessimism. . . . Perhaps to understand the optimism of Assis one needs only to be a realist, a hard, pragmatic realist. . . ."[20]

Often, as in his brilliantly satirical "Psychiatrist," Machado's method is ironic, getting his reader to think about emulating not the actions he or she is reading about but the opposite of those actions. Do not, he implies in "Alexandrine Tale," "The Psychiatrist," and "Lição de botânica," trust science to be a panacea for the woes of the human race and do not be misled into believing that wealth, privilege, and social status necessarily lead to moral behavior. In sum, Machado's social conscience is a logical extension of his too infrequently appreciated faith in the importance of willpower, rational choice, and generosity in the conduct of our lives. Basically stoic and existentialist in his concept of life, and like Camus possessed of a conscience that, for better or worse, linked the reality of the individual existence to larger social and political issues, Machado de Assis was a writer whose most basic themes are the eternal ones that philosophically question the nature of human existence. An artist whose version of the human experience transcended his own time and place, Machado de Assis is at once the most Brazilian of writers and the most universal.

Chapter Four
Style and Technique

As critics have long noted, Machado de Assis writes with a very distinctive style. Clear, concise, and classically serene in its precision and economy of means, Machado's manner of presentation is unmistakable. For all its calmly rational and ironic detachment, however, Machado's basic prose style creates a fictive world that is often regarded as nihilistic and despairing. There is a sharp discordance between Machado's use of cool, melodious prose to convey messages of deeply unsettling import. Far from superficial adornment, Machado's style, ironic, imagistic, and succinct, is an integral part of his artistic expression.

On close examination Machado's highly refined prose reveals a style that is profoundly epistemic, an organic extension of his own sense of what reality is like and how it could be best represented in art. Like Flaubert Machado was a meticulous craftsman, a writer for whom the quest for the mot juste was an all-pervading concern. Yet, Machado was also like Joyce in his deliberate mixing, metaphorically and metonymically, of the modes of both realism and symbolism. The semantic dimension of Machado's fiction, therefore, is essentially a function of what Suzanne Langer calls "presentational symbolism," that is, a manner of writing whose symbols "are involved in a simultaneous, integral presentation."[1] By focusing our attention not merely on what Machado says but on how he says it, we can see the epistemological and aesthetic choices the Brazilian master made in the creation of his highly identifiable art.

One of the most fundamental dimensions of a writer's style is diction, the characteristic word choices that he or she makes. Machado had a definite predilection for simple language, for words that, though carefully selected and used with economy and precision, are not in and of themselves ornate, erudite, or otherwise "difficult." His use of Portuguese, moreover, tends to be nineteenth-century Brazilian, reflecting the usages of middle-class men and women of his time and place.[2]

Barreto Filho, a noted Brazilian critic who has specialized in stylistic approaches to Machado's work, also observes, however, that Machado's stylistic singularity arises from his skill at integrating certain forms of classical Portuguese with new Brazilian usages, especially those of the "Carioca," or resident of Rio de Janeiro, Machado's own lifelong home.[3] Yet even in Machado's early work, his theater and poetry as well as his prose, there is a pronounced preference for unadorned language and for nonsesquipedalian words. The opening lines of "Miss Dollar" (the initial selection in *Contos fluminenses,* Machado's first collection of stories), for example, are:

If the reader is a young man and inclined to a melancholy outlook he will imagine that Miss Dollar is a pale and slender English girl, one scant of both flesh and blood, whose two great blue eyes open up a flower of a face and whose long blond braids tremble in the wind. The girl in question should be as vaporous and idealized as one of Shakespeare's creations; she should be the opposite of English roastbeef. Tea and milk should be the basic foodstuffs of such a creature, who might also consume some candies and cookies in order to succor the urgencies of the stomach. Her speech should a murmur of an Aeolian harp; . . .
The image is poetic, but it's not that of the heroine of the story.[4]

Even here, at this early point in his career, Machado is employing a diction that, though simple and clear, is capable of creating sharply drawn and ironically charged images that imply considerably more than they state denotatively. Apparent here, too, is Machado's usage of erudite allusions (one of the most notable aspects of his style) and his knack for drawing ironic contrasts between the sublime (Aeolian harps, for example) and the quotidian (the physical description of Miss Dollar). Machado employs no difficult or complex words in this description of what, ironically, Miss Dollar is not. Words like "stomach," "scant," and "braids," indeed, typify demotic (rather than hieratic, or self-consciously "literary") style, which Northrop Frye discusses in *The Well-Tempered Critic* (1963).

This simplicity of language is by no means limited to Machado's early work, however; functioning in consort with Machado's frequent and strategic use of learned allusions, it is fully characteristic of his later work as well. In two of his most famous poems he speaks of "a blue fly" ("Uma môsca azul") and "a vicious circle" ("Círculo vicioso") and in *Dom Casmurro,* his most sophisticated and complex novel, he employs chapters with headings such as, "The Title," "The Book," "The Worms," "The Homeric Heifer," "The Portrait," "The Cup of Coffee," and "A Tardy Question." As structuralist and poststructuralist critics like Roland Barthes, Jacques Derrida, Julia Kristeva, Gaston Bachelard, Georges Poulet, and Jonathan Culler remind us, however, the "simple" diction of a philosophically oriented writer like Machado de Assis often amounts to a mask, which serves ironically to heighten the reader's apprehension of the complexities involved in the text's generation of meanings. Though simple in terms of its diction, Machado's style is highly complex in terms of what Derrida would call its "différance," the fluid interplay of ideas and structures with which it deals.

Closely related to the question of word choice is that of syntax, the structure of the typical Machadoan sentence. Standing in sharp contrast to the lengthy compound-complex sentences so frequently used by James, Machado's sentences tend to be basically short, simple, frequently compound or complex but rarely compound-complex like those of the late James. With their fundamentally simple diction and syntax, Machado's sentences are both comically disarming in their effect on the reader and discomfiting in their subtle presentation of such disturbing ontological issues as the transitoriness of human existence, the corrosive effect of time, and the ambivalence of human motivation. Suggestive and evocative, as in poetry, rather than what Roman Jakobson describes as metonymically declarative, Machado's syntax is, "simple, exact, clear, [with] a 'brisé' rhythm, 'saccadé,' short phrases, discontinuous, spotted, devoid of 'élan' and oratorical effects, fragmented, without symmetry, without subordinations and coordinations."[5]

Like Proust in *A Rememberance of Things Past,* Machado evokes the past and renders it a vital, living force in the present by means of a consistent use of what Coutinho calls the "imperfeito narrativo," or "narrative imperfect," a past time verb tense that, as Meyer says, "phases into the present, an astonishing psychological present and not a simple imitation of the historical present."[6] Examples of this syntactical simplicity, one that frames and at the same time enhances or expands a complex idea, abound in Machado's work. In *Epitaph of a Small Winner,* for example, the narrator Braz Cubas jots down in chapter 119 six of his personal maxims, concepts that he himself, perhaps to mislead the reader from making a critical observation about his character, describes as "yawns born of boredom" (207). Simple in language and sentence structure but profound in meaning, these deceptive maxims paint a devastating picture of Braz, in which he, unintentionally the reader feels, wryly reveals himself to be an egoist and a cynic and to have lived a kind of death in life. As Braz breezily but chillingly avers, "One endures with patience the pain in the other fellow's stomach"; "We kill time; time buries us"; and "Believe in yourself, but do not always refuse to believe in others" (207). In a later scene, when Braz and Quincas Borba happen upon a dogfight, Quincas, the ostensibly "mad" philosopher, observes that "in some parts of the world the spectacle is more grandiose: human creatures fight with dogs for bones and for other even less appetizing dishes—a struggle greatly complicated by the use of human intelligence with all the accumulation of wisdom that man has received through the centuries, etc." (230). Though it is not immediately apparent from reading these unadorned, straightforward, and syntactically uncomplicated lines, what Machado succeeds in doing here is sardonically to equate human existence with a savage dogfight. The philosophically complex implications of this equation, which are expressed implicitly through the reader's active participation in the formulation of the text's potential meanings, stand in ironic contrast to the simplicity of the expression's diction and syntax. As is apparent from a close reading of this representative passage, what is literally said in Machado's texts is seldom all that is meant.

Also clearly demonstrated in his subtle insinuation that human existence is a dogfight, one sadly in which we use our celebrated "intelligence" to intensify the fight (rather than to eliminate the need to fight), over "dishes" even "less appetizing" than bones, is Machado's effective use of figurative language to structure his texts and advance their plots. Indeed, Machado's use of images, symbols, similes, metaphors, and other tropes is so extensive and so permeates his work that one is led to conclude that he writes prose as if he were writing poetry. Since the essence of Machado's economical style is nuance, or subtle, often ironic suggestions and comparisons, rather than protracted realistic description or explicit authorial commentary, one is not surprised to discover his great affinity for figurative language. What is singular is the extent to which Machado employs a variety of often highly original images, tropes, and figures. Also notable is the deftness with which he patterns these into powerful designs within his work and with which he makes them, and not external action (of which there is very little), advance his artfully contrived plots. As critics like Gomes, Coutinho, Caldwell, Nunes, and others have noted, Machado's concept of art was often less realistic than symbolic and, especially in certain later works like *Esau and Jacob* and *Counselor Ayres' Memorial,* increasingly mythic.[7]

Working in the tradition of Aristotle, Machado saw art not as copying nature but as "imitating" it, transforming and transfiguring it, through the use of symbols and interrelated images, into a new and more enduring form of reality. By larding his sprightly texts with allusions to other works, authors, and characters of Western culture and literature, Machado like Jorge Luis Borges achieves for his work an intertextual range and resonance it would otherwise not have had. It is through this same mechanism of using allusions that Machado like Eliot establishes an ironic and contrastive function for his own themes and personages. When, for example, in *Epitaph of a Small Winner* Quincas Borba declares that "Pangloss . . . was not so great a fool as Voltaire thought" (206), he is making an ironic comment that elicits from the reader a careful consideration both of Pangloss's function in *Candide* and of the several possible implications Pangloss's character might have in terms of possible comparisons with Quincas Borba's role (or Braz Cubas's role) in *Epitaph of a Small Winner*. And later, when Braz, hoping to advance himself politically, considers marriage to a humble girl, he decides, using a metaphor that tellingly suggests both his arrogant and egotistical nature, "There is no alternative; . . . I must pluck this flower from the swamp" (211). A final and famous example of Machado's metaphoric style occurs in chapter 71, when Braz, having just accused the reader of being the book's "great defect," whimsically compares the style and structure of his text to the way a pair of drunks walk. Speaking metafictively to his reader, Braz avers, "You want to live fast, to get to the end, and the book ambles along slowly; you like straight, solid narrative and a smooth style, but this book and my style are like a pair of drunks: they stagger to the right and to the left, they start and they stop, they mutter, they roar, they guffaw, they threaten the sky, they slip and fall" (143).

Although it is a constant force in his work, Machado's use of figurative language reaches a peak in *Dom Casmurro,* a novel whose plot is intensified and pushed ineluctably forward less by action than by a complex pattern of closely interwoven symbols and images. While virtually every chapter develops around and through some particular image or allusion, the novel's basic metaphoric structure rests on an evolving and ultimately tragic relationship between the following imagistically rendered chapters: 1, "The title"; 2, "The book"; 9, "The opera"; 32, "Eyes like the tide"; 33, "The combing of the braids"; 55, "A sonnet"; 73, "The stage manager"; 83, "The portrait"; 123, "Eyes like the tide"; 132, "The sketch and the color"; 135, "Othello"; and 148, "Well, and the rest?" In terms of their internal relationships, these core chapters resonate semantically within each other, following the metaphoric principle of similarity and substitution in the following ways: chapter 1, "The title," prefigures chapter 148, "Well, and the rest?"; chapter 2 does the same for chapter 55; chapter 9 parallels chapter 73; chapter 32 is reenacted (to a heightened effect) in chapter 123; chapter 33 pairs off in ironic (and tragic) contrast to chapter 135; and, in one of the novel's most crucial metaphoric linkages, chapter 83, "The portrait," anticipates chapter 132, "The sketch and the color," the section of the narrative that functions as its turning point.

Applying Jakobson's theory about metaphor and metonymy to Machado's prose style, it becomes clear that Machado de Assis, like other modern narrativists, such as Joyce, Virginia Woolf, and Gertrude Stein, tends toward metaphoric, rather than metonymic, expression. For Jakobson, the language of realism hews closer to the contiguous relationships, in language and reality, of metonymy while that of romanticism and symbolism is more characterized by metaphor and metaphoric relationships. Although Machado, like Joyce, certainly makes use of both metaphor and metonymy, a close reading of novels like *Epitaph of a Small Winner, Philosopher or Dog?, Dom Casmurro, Esau and Jacob,* stories like "A Woman's Arms," "The Looking Glass," "The Secret Heart," "Alexandrian Tale," "A Canary's Ideas," "Funeral March," and "Pylades and Orestes," poems like "A Creature," "Vicious Circle," and "Blue Fly," and dramas like "Quase ministro," "Os deuses de casaca," and "Lição de botânica" reveals a strong preference on Machado's part for metaphor, the typically modernist mode of expression, over metonymy, the characteristic mode (according to Jakobson) of realism. The interiorized conflicts of novels like *Dom Casmurro,* and *Epitaph of a Small Winner,* for example, are "forwarded" much more by metaphor than by metonymy.[8] In *Epitaph of a Small Winner,* to cite only one of this key novel's numerous examples of the technique, Machado, consistent with one of his most fundamental thematic concerns, casts chapter 8, "Reason versus Folly," in the image of a verbal and physical struggle between these two comically personified forces for control of human activity. And, even the chapter headings of *Dom Casmurro,* which are woven together on the principle of similarity and substitution, are generally more metaphoric than realistic. Indeed, as in *Ulysses,* the dominant point of view of *Dom Casmurro* (the text of which is the interiorized autobiography of the main character, Dom Casmurro) proceeds largely—and decisively—on the strength of similarities, substitutions, and repetitions perceived or alleged by the protagonist. When, for example, Dom Casmurro contemplates, in chapter 2, the house he has built as an old man, which he hopes will replicate his childhood home, he begins metaphorically to establish for the reader an analogy with what he later says (chap. 55) about a certain sonnet, whose middle lines were never completed. In both cases, metaphorically speaking, something is missing, a mysterious "absence" or "something" that in the course of the novel shows itself to be nothing less than life itself, a life wasted by a man who allows himself to be overcome by envy, jealousy, and self-doubt. Though they have different reasons for doing so, both Leopold Bloom in *Ulysses* and Dom Casmurro move their respective narratives by perceiving things both as they are and through analogies with other things, "real" and imagined.

Indeed, the entire plot of *Dom Casmurro* turns on just such a metaphorically rendered recurrence, in this case one involving chapters 83 and 132: when, in chapter 132, "The sketch and the color" (which, like chap. 83, involves a problem of resemblance) the narrator looks more and more intensely at his son's face, it suddenly occurs to him that the child looks so much like his friend Escobar that he must, he decides, be his. Combining, as the modernists do, synecdochic details (synecdoche being closely related to metonymy) with metaphoric substitution or analogy, the narrator of *Dom Casmurro,* ruminating imagistically in a kind of free association (one similar to the "talking cure" described by Freud in many of his case studies) upon the physical object he has just perceived, declares, "Escobar emerged from the grave, from the seminary, from Flamengo; he sat at table with me, welcomed me on the stairs, kissed me each morning in my study or asked for the customary blessing at night. All this repelled me" (239). While, as David Lodge observes, a novel like Joyce's *Finnegans Wake* is based entirely on the metaphoric principle of similarity and substitution, *Dom Casmurro* is, as we can see in the recurring metaphoric interrelationships between the chapters, a narrative in which virtually "every event is a re-enactment or a premonition of several other events. . . ."[9] In sum, Machado's extensive and systematic utilization of figurative language is an extraordinary feature of his work.

Integrally bound up in the issue of style, the question of technique is important to understanding how Machado achieves his artistic ends. Always critically aware of his own work, Machado, whose theories about the nature of literary art were markedly eclectic, was ahead of his time in his numerous experiments with such basics of narrative as the presentation and development of characters, the nature and development of plot, the structuring of secondary conflicts, the handling of time, the selection of a point (or points) of view to tell the story, and the potentialities inherent in the metafictive use of narratees and of self-conscious but often unreliable first-person narrators, many of whom, like Braz Cubas and Dom Casmurro, are the protagonists of their own stories. In *Counselor Ayres' Memorial,* by way of contrast, the narrator Ayres is not centrally involved in the action he relates and his perception is limited to the events he has witnessed. And in novels like *Philosopher or Dog?* and *Ressurreição* the narrative voice is omniscient and comments freely on all aspects of the narrative, including the psychological states and motives of the characters. Yet, as Meyer believes, in all of these diverse works the common and therefore dominant feature remains Machado's innovative experiment with point of view, his tendency as a psychological narrativist to superimpose, often to ironic or ambiguous effect, a subjective on an objective view.[10] In general, Machado's highly diverse approach to the crucial question of point of view constitutes, as with James, one of his most enduring contributions to the development of narrative.

Other notable technical features of Machado's art include his innovative use of satire, irony, and ironic contrast; his concept of plot as a psychological issue arising out of a conflict between will, intention, or interest within a single human mind; his penchant for using comic and even absurdist situations to make implicit statements about the tragic nature of human existence; his use of self-conscious and unreliable narrators; his skill at creating fascinating and compelling characters, male as well as female; and his experiments with the creation of metafictional texts that John Barth has called postmodernistic in their tone, critical self-consciousness, and flaunting of their own artifice.[11]

A "terrifying" satirist, one less merciful even than Swift, "in his exposure of the pretentiousness and the hypocrisy that lurk in the average good man and woman,"[12] Machado, as seen in works like "The Psychiatrist," "The Bonzo's Secret," "Alexandrian Tale," and *Epitaph of a Small Winner,* is nevertheless widely regarded as a comic writer, one for whom humor, typically of a mordant, ironic variety, is also a technical device used to incisive satirical effect. In *Epitaph of a Small Winner,* for example, Machado pillories the then popular philosophy of positivism, which he loathed, by having one of his major characters, the insane "philosopher," Quincas Borba, promote an absurd philosophical system of his own creation that he calls "Humanitism." A withering parody of Auguste Comte's positivism and potentially at least a satirical rendering of both Leibnitz[13] and Nietzsche (in particular his "superman" theory), humanitism is a philosophy of total egoism, one that claims (as Comte claimed for his theory) to be unassailably based in "scientific" rationale. Another example of Machado's skill at metaphoric development and repetition, the chapter devoted to humanitism (chap. 117) is an elaborate thematic extension of chapter 7, "The Delirium," the section that comically yet terrifyingly posits that it is human fate to live a rapacious and egotistical existence within an utterly indifferent and ambivalent universe. In terms of its effect on the reader, Machado's humor first gets us to laugh but then, after a moment's reflection about why we are laughing, it leads us to contemplate seriously the frustrating enigma of human existence, which is the thematic fount of Machado's art.

Another of Machado's key technical devices has to do with his sense of plot structure, of what constitutes narrative plotting and how it can be developed. Appearing in embryonic theoretical form as early as the preface to his first novel, *Ressurreição* (1872), but receiving a detailed articulation in his 1878 criticism both of Eça de Queirós's *Cousin Basilio* and of French naturalism in general, Machado's concept is that a novel's plot should be based not on any external action or event (though these may influence the plot) but on conflicts within the characters themselves. This distinctly psychological, or "interiorized," concept of narrative plot, one that also makes him seem more of a twentieth- than a nineteenth-century writer, is a constant feature of Machado's fiction. Nowhere is it more vividly displayed, however, than in

Epitaph of a Small Winner and *Dom Casmurro,* the two great novels of his mature phase. By employing both temporal and structural disjunctions, and by giving his novels what appears to be (but is decidedly not) a randomly episodic structure, Machado, as early as 1880, was writing a very modernistic kind of narrative, in which temporal dislocation played a key role. In *Epitaph of a Small Winner,* for example, he begins with a narrator who is discussing the circumstances surrounding his death, while in *Dom Casmurro* he withholds the denouement until virtually the end of the novel, when the narrator basically orders the reader to accept his version of what has happened. As metaphorically expressed in chapters like 23, "Sad but Short"; 24, "Short but Happy"; 26, "The Author is Undecided"; 31, "The Black Butterfly"; 79, "The Compromise"; and 160, "Negatives" (all from *Epitaph of a Small Winner,*) and in chapters like 2, "The book"; 37, "The soul is full of mysteries"; 54, "Panegyric of Saint Monica"; 75, "Despair"; 105, "Arms"; 137, "Second impulse"; and 146, "No leprosy" (from *Dom Casmurro*), we see that the basic conflicts of two of Machado's most famous novels are essentially psychological in nature. Epitomizing Machado's belief that a novel's plot should derive from the conflicts within the mind of a single character, Braz Cubas's and Dom Casmurro's greatest struggles, like those of better known modernist heroes, are with their own ambivalent and inconsistent natures.

What is unique about Machado's handling of his metaphysical and ontological themes is that he presents them comically. In work after work we see Machado using comic scenes and situations to lead us to serious philosophic reflection about the nature of human existence. In *Epitaph of a Small Winner,* for example, the chapter metaphorically entitled "The Black Butterfly" (31) is at once a whimsical and ironic but finally sad parable about the relationship between the human creature and God. Letting a butterfly represent the human being, Braz himself (ironically) God ("the maker of butterflies"), and life "the adventure" (which is capriciously ended by God), Machado presents a masterfully succinct scene that powerfully states the absurdly tragicomic essence of the human condition: "The butterfly had probably come out of the woods, well-fed and happy, into the sunlight of a beautiful morning. . . . It flew through my open window, entered my room, and found me there. . . . Then it said to itself, 'This is probably the maker of butterflies.' The idea overwhelmed it, terrified it. . . . When I brushed it away . . . a towel ended the adventure" (87).

This same teleological concern appears in *Dom Casmurro,* whose narrator, Dom Casmurro, comically equates life to an opera in which God supplies the words and Satan the music. Equally attracted by these conflicting desires (God's words and Satan's music), the human creature experiences anxiety, confusion, and frustration. Clearly apparent in stories like "A Second Life," "Adam and Eve," "A Canary's Ideas," and "Funeral March," and in poems like "The Blue Fly" and "Vicious Circle," this technique of couching serious philosophic speculation in comic language looms large among Machado's most distinctive stylistic features.

A fourth outstanding technical attribute of Machado's art is, as Nunes points out, characterization, especially his innovative experiments with self-conscious and fallible narrator/protagonists, both male and female.[14] Although, as Robert Alter shows in *Partial Magic,* self-conscious narrative is by no means a new phenomenon, it is revealing of Machado's excellence as an experimental narrativist to evaluate his works in the tradition Alter discusses, one that includes such well-known figures as Cervantes, Sterne, Stendhal, Fielding, Denis Diderot, Woolf, André Gide, Miguel de Unamuno, Kafka, Joyce, Mann, Borges, Samuel Beckett, Vladimir Nabokov, and Barth, among others.[15]

Other than his utilization of self-conscious narrators like Braz Cubas and Dom Casmurro, Machado's characters can be divided with respect to their technical development, as João Ribeiro suggests, into two groups: those that are presented by being described and those that, in what is often called the "dramatic method," present themselves through their own actions and comments.[16] As Ribeiro and others have noted, Machado is particularly adept at handling the "dramatic method" of character presentation, a feature of his work increasingly prominent in the post-1880 stories. Driven by complex and conflicting psychological forces, and often possessed of an acute, if frequently duplicitous, self-consciousness, Machado's most memorable fictional men and women are simultaneously attractive and repellent.

Closely related to Machado's use of self-conscious narrators are his numerous experiments with the creation of metafictional texts, which make the nature of their own composition one of their chief subjects. Machado, whom John Barth has termed a "proto-post-modernist" because of his long love affair with self-consciously critical narratives, began in earnest to cultivate this mode of writing only after 1880.[17] It is this metafictional element that is perhaps the first technical feature of *Epitaph of a Small Winner* to catch the reader's eye. Machado opens this 1880 novel with the narrator/protagonist Braz Cubas speaking directly to the reader about the extraordinary nature of the work he has written: "The book must suffice in itself; if it please you excellent reader, I shall be rewarded for my labor; if it please you not, I shall reward you with a snap of my fingers and good riddance to you" (17–18). Braz Cubas maintains this stance of "authorial" self-scrutiny throughout his text, with chapters 34, "To a Sensitive Soul"; 55, "The Venerable Dialogue of Adam and Eve"; 71, "The Defect of This Book"; 98, "Deleted"; and 99, "In the Pit," being particularly exemplary of his technique. Through Braz Cubas, Machado slyly suggests a playful yet despairing attitude about the relationship between life and literary art that is akin to the one implicit in the essays in William Gass's book *Fiction and the Figures of Life* (1971). Like Gass, Braz Cubas (Machado de Assis) realizes that a writer does not realistically render or present a world; rather, he or she creates one symbolically by means of the elusive and unstable medium of language, which itself constitutes a fluid symbolic system. Machado's metafictional self-awareness is not limited to his fiction, however. Appearing in such poems as the parodic mock epic, "O Almada" (which parodies both Homer and Luís de Camões), the sonnet, "Sonêto de Natal," and the ironic "Pálida Elvira," this same critical self-awareness permeates his work, extending even into his nonfiction. One of Machado's unmistakable trademarks, this artistic self-consciousness offers the reader insight into not only the themes he developed but also the function of the sundry styles, forms, and techniques he used. In his poetry and especially in his later prose Machado made considerable use of metafictional texts in an attempt to get the reader actively involved in the creation of the text's meaning. By making the reader a participant in the construction of his metaphoric and symbolic narratives, Machado was once again proving himself to be well in advance of his time, a fact that may help explain the consternation and confusion many critics felt in reading his post-1880 works when they were first published.

Whether in his clear, concise, and always economical style or in his experiments with such narrative concerns as plot, structure, irony, point of view, and characterization, Machado de Assis proved himself to be the consummate master craftsman. In the best tradition of Flaubert, James, and Joyce, Machado helped raise narrative art to new levels of sophistication and excellence.

Chapter Five
The Novels

Although Machado de Assis worked extensively in poetry, drama, and nonfictional prose, it was unquestionably in fiction that he achieved his greatest triumphs. And while he is best known outside of Brazil as a novelist, probably because all his novels save one, *Ressurreição,* have been translated, he is widely regarded by a number of discerning critics as an even more accomplished short story writer. But whether it was in the compact, demanding story form or the longer, more flexible novel form, Machado was always a writer for whom the art of fiction was the highest priority. As a fledgling writer, Machado had worked primarily in poetry, publishing his first original composition, a short poem, "Ela" (She) in 1855.[1] By the mid to late 1860s, however, he had come more and more to cultivate narrative fiction, a genre in which he later emerged as one of the great masters of his era.[2]

In his lifetime Machado de Assis wrote nine novels and produced seven collections of short stories, in addition to a great many stories that never appeared in book form.[3] His first novel, the relatively simple but engaging *Ressurreição* (1872), is not, as the preface makes clear, a novel of manners but rather a psychological character study, one based on two conflicting attitudes—a desire to love and a propensity for cynicism—held simultaneously within the mind of the protagonist, a secure middle-class man named Felix. The novel's title "Resurrection" reflects a typically Machadoan touch of irony concerning the fate of the main character, Felix, however. While Felix's moribund capacity to give and receive love is indeed for a time "resurrected" by Livia, his female counterpart, it is eventually snuffed out by his crippling doubts, fears, and jealousy. Though not fully depicted as such, Felix has the potential to be a truly tragic character, one whose overwhelming, "refusal to yield . . . typifies the Sophoclean hero."[4] Prototypical of Machado's greatest characters, Felix is his own worst enemy.

Ressurreição fails to be the powerful tragedy it could have been, however, because Felix's tragic dimension is mitigated by the active presence of several other important characters, most notably the loving and romantically idealized Livia and the essentially comic figures of Clara, Menezes (Felix's loyal friend), Vianna, and Baptista, the latter "a plain-dealing villain like Don John of *Much Ado About Nothing*."[5]

Thematically, *Ressurreição* initiates one of Machado's most recurring and fundamental issues, one given truly tragic rendition in *Dom Casmurro:* the effects of living a life in which the redeeming urge to love is defeated by the simultaneously existent urge not to love, not to give of oneself, not to trust in others. Utilizing in crude form the metaphoric style that distinguished the subtle narratives of his later period, Machado's implied author (who speaks openly and often to the reader) concludes *Ressurreição* by likening Felix to a dying flame: "O amor extinguiu-se como lâmpada a que faltou óleo. Era a convivência da moça que lhe nutría a chama. Quando ela desapareceu, a chama exausta expirou" (The love was extinguished like a lamp lacking oil. It was his acquaintanceship with the girl that had fed the flame. When she disappeared, the flame, exhausted, went out).[6] The first of Machado's brilliant gallery of self-destructing protagonists, Felix, who, as Nunes notes, is successfully drawn by means of both extensive summary and narrative analysis, fails to control the ruinously negative impulses that lead him to allow cynicism, doubt, fear, and jealousy to win out over love.[7] Machado's sense of the reader's active rather than passive role in the appreciation of Felix's failure to love is vital to a complete critical estimation of his novel. Moreover, it also shows how as early as 1872 Machado, ever the individualist, was experimenting with different dimensions of the intrusive omniscient narrator at a time when such writers as Flaubert and James, "were insisting on the 'disappearance' of the narrator."[8]

Standing in sharp contrast to the tragic potential *of Ressurreição,* Machado's second novel, *The Hand and the Glove* (1874), is basically a romantic comedy replete with happy ending. While in the first novel we see the failure of love, which results in a hollow existence (this being a major motif of Machado's work), in the second novel we have the victory of love. When in the conclusion the two intelligent, strong-willed and illusion-free lovers, Guiomar and Luis, decide to marry, the clear and entirely felicitous implication is that in pledging themselves to each other, and in maintaining a close control over their emotions and conflicting desires, they will achieve a loving and harmonious union, one in which, as metaphorically expressed in the title, they will fit together "like a hand in a glove." Reminiscent of Stendhal's *Rouge et le noir* in that it concerns itself with clear-minded action, determination, and strength of will, *The Hand in the Glove* implies that in spite of what Machado may have believed about the ultimate futility of human endeavor, he also felt a need for decisive action and willpower in life. He suggests here and elsewhere that whatever happiness we human beings can attain we must take steps to facilitate. This healthy, nonromanticized view of love surfaces as the basic thematic concern in what is otherwise a lightly satiric love story. Strength of will, resolution and ambition, and a sober understanding of what it means to love another human being, win out over vanity and a fatuously romantic view of love and life.

Machado's third novel, *Helena* (1876), which may have directly influenced Eça de Queirós's *Maias*, "marks a big step forward in Assis's early avowed artistic purpose of presenting the drama resulting from the emotional conflicts of his characters."[9] Composed of often conflicting traces of tragedy, comedy, satire, melodrama, and romance, this novel, which still numbers among Machado's most popular works, fails to become the powerfully focused work of art its numerous finely wrought elements, such as its potentially tragic conflict and its more complex characters, suggest it could have been. Merging social concerns, such as class consciousness, the marriage of convenience, and incest,[10] with such psychological issues as pride, love, and willpower, *Helena* is technically a step forward for Machado because of its greatly increased use of a subdued but powerful symbolism, one that itself subtly forwards the action. Presenting an acute consciousness of the passage of time and of its destructive effect on human affairs, *Helena,* like the two novels that preceded it, implicitly advocates the inherent superiority—for human beings and their chances for happiness—of subjective, Bergsonian time over external or chronological time.

A final signal feature of *Helena* is that its narrator is both less glaringly intrusive than in the earlier novels and less prolix in terms of the comments he makes. As Nunes notes, referring to *Helena's* narrator, "Although he refers to himself as 'I,' is omniscient, enters the characters' consciousness at will, and engages frequently in narrative analysis of motives, he withholds complete knowledge from the reader in order to preserve mystery. . . . His comments, however, are limited and unexuberant in comparison with those of Machado de Assis's previous novels."[11]

The fourth and final novel of Machado's so-called "early phase" is *Iaiá Garcia* (1878), a work widely regarded as the most complete artistic accomplishment of his pre-1880 period. While *Iaiá Garcia* continues to employ the unifying symbolism that had so distinguished *Helena,* its outstanding characteristic, as many critics have observed, is the central role it gives to time. As with Proust's *Remembrance of Things Past,* time can be said to be the main character of *Iaiá Garcia,* the one whose constant presence affects all the others. As in the earlier novels, *Iaiá Garcia's* rather complicated plot rests basically on a love affair, though in this case it is a triangular one involving two women, Iaiá Garcia and Estela, and a man, Jorge, with whom they are both involved. Like *The Hand and the Glove* and *Helena, Iaiá Garcia* is sociological in that it suggests that to marry for any reason other than love, a marriage of convenience, for example, is to debase everyone involved. More acutely class-conscious than its predecessor, *Helena, Iaiá Garcia* also involves a by now characteristic theme of Machado de Assis: the struggle between conflicting motivations within a single human soul. As depicted in the figure of Estela, another of Machado's extraordinary female portraits, this struggle here shows itself to be between love and pride, between Estela's ability to love another person and her justifiable sense of personal integrity and worth. Although Estela is a typical Machadoan character in that her pride ultimately overpowers the love that also animates her "warm, almost passionate nature,"[12] she is unique in that this same pride becomes for her not a crippling liability that stunts her healthy psychological development but an asset, one that Machado, by means of a positive allusion to Italian poet Torquato Tasso, expresses metaphorically through the image of a shield: "Her pride did not emanate from impotent envy or sterile ambition; it was a force, not a vice; it was her buckler of diamonds—that which preserved her from ills, as that of Tasso's angel who defended chaste and saintly cities."[13] Although Machado's first four novels became progressively more complex and sophisticated as works of art, their real importance, as many have observed, can only be appreciated when compared to the great narratives that came later. Nevertheless, the careful reader can discern in Machado's pre-1880 novels an ever increasing concern with character development and with technique, as well as the iconoclasm, eclecticism, and originality that marked his later works.[14]

The first of these "later works," and perhaps the best known of all Machado's novels, is the extraordinary *Epitaph of a Small Winner* (1880, serialized edition; 1881, book form), some six chapters of which, owing to Machado's deteriorating eyesight, were dictated to his wife, Carolina. Yet when one undertakes a close critical reading of all Machado's novels, it becomes easier to understand why Afrânio Coutinho believes that it is only a "false dichotomy" that separates the early from the later Machado.[15] But while one can accept Coutinho's argument that the supposed "new aesthetic" of the post-1880 works is in truth the logical result of a process of artistic experimentation and development that had been going on for years and that can be traced back through the earlier works, the appearance of the dramatically different *Epitaph of a Small Winner* must still be regarded as a stunning moment in Machado's artistic growth. The elusively polysemic relationship between Braz Cubas, the novel's narrator/protagonist, and his readers (or listeners) epitomizes what Gérard Genette has in mind when, discussing the narratee, he writes, "The true author of the narrative is not only the one who recounts it but also, and sometimes even more so, the one who listens to it."[16] Also reflecting the essential modernity of this partially anachronistic 1880 narrative is the fluid involvement between Braz Cubas, the reader, and what Iser, Genette, Stanley Fish, and others call the "implied reader." Further complicated by being the first-person tale of a fallible, ironic, and cannily self-conscious narrator, the story Braz relates in *Epitaph of a Small Winner* opens itself up to an infinite number of readings and interpretations. Traditionally, Braz Cubas has been more or less identified with Machado himself, although because of Machado's own admonition against taking this biographical approach to his texts and because there is no necessary connection between them, it seems prudent, as Sandra Messinger Cypess shows, to separate what Braz Cubas says from what Machado himself stood for.[17] This disparity between Braz's system of values and those by which Machado lived his life is clearly seen in chapter 24, "Short but Happy," when Braz frankly emphasizes his superficiality, his mediocrity and his lack of any deeply held convictions: "To tell the whole truth, my beliefs reflected those of a barber whom I had patronized in Modena and who was distinguished by the fact that he had no beliefs. . . . Perhaps the reader is astonished by the frankness with which I expose and emphasize my mediocrity; let him remember that frankness is the virtue most appropriate to a defunct" (74). Using a visit to a barbershop to symbolize, ironically, his personal world view, Braz defines here himself as a shallow and ostentatious hypocrite, a condition in no way applicable to the real Machado de Assis. Braz's (Machado's) creation of several implied readers is similarly apparent throughout his narrative. In chapter 49, "The Tip of the Nose," for example, he addresses his reader both affectionately, as in "beloved reader," and critically, as in "obtuse reader." And later, in chapter 71, "The Defect of This Book," Braz comically charges the reader with being the book's major "problem": "the great defect of this book is you, reader" (143).

Thematically, *Epitaph of a Small Winner* projects a more elaborate and telling condemnation of self-love than *Ressurreição*. It should be noted, however, that while this theme is a very serious one in terms of Machado's overall career, and although it is cast sadly and fatalistically by Braz, the overall tone of Braz's posthumous memoirs vacillates between the pathetic and the comic. As is characteristic in his mature art, Machado, working through his independent, fallible, and self-conscious narrator/protagonists and his various implied readers, leads us to laugh at—and perhaps eventually think about—issues of immense moral and ethical seriousness, issues of choice and conduct that determine who and what we are in our transient existences. By allowing Braz to so ardently and unremorsefully reflect on a life based utterly on egoism, or self-love, Machado (through Braz) is indirectly suggesting that what Braz achieved or represented in life may not have been as wonderful as he implies it was, that the reader of his memoirs might decide to live by a different moral and ethical code of conduct, one based on love of others rather than egoism.

In *Philosopher or Dog?* (1891), Machado returns, though in an amplified fashion, to his great theme of love versus self-love. The novel's protagonist, the humble school teacher, Rubião, has inherited the dog and the ideas of Quincas Borba, a character who had appeared in the previous novel, *Epitaph of a Small Winner,* as the mad exponent of humanitism, a philosophy that, parodically echoing Nietzsche's "superman" theory and ridiculing Comte's positivism, was based on egoism and a Darwin-like concept of the survival of the fittest. Although *Philosopher or Dog?* can be considered technically less innovative than its immediate predecessor (primarily because it relies more on a third-person omniscient narrator than on a self-conscious first-person one), it constitutes a more sophisticated structural achievement because it effectively entwines Machado's bedrock theme, the individual's eternal struggle between love of others and self-love, with a symbolically rendered social dimension and with a more complex sense of characterization. As Nunes says, "Society's values are the same as Quincas Borba's, mad and egotistical," and tragically it is the essentially decent but fatally confused Rubião's inability to discern the cancerous conflict between love and self-love raging within his own soul that leads to his madness and death.[18] At the very outset of the novel an image invokes another key Machadoan theme, the changes wrought by the passage of time, brilliantly illustrating the "abyss" between the human heart and mind, that is, between one's conscious and unconscious desires. Machado's narrator metaphorically lays out the as yet unrecognized conflict that eventually destroys the unsuspecting Rubião: regard for others versus love of self.[19]

> Rubião was gazing at the bay. . . . He was comparing the past with the present. . . . What an abyss there is between the mind and the heart! The ex-teacher's mind, displeased with that thought recoiled, sought something else to think about, a small boat that was going by; the heart, however, allowed itself to beat joyously. What did it care about the boat, or the boatman. . . . It, the heart, was saying that since Sister Piedade had to die, it was well that she did not marry; there might have been a son or daughter.—A pretty boat!—It was better so!—How well the man bends to the oars!—One thing certain is that they are in Heaven!
> (3–4).

As Rubião's unchecked "heart" exults in thinking about the material possessions he has inherited (and that he now covets), his rational, guilt-ridden, conscious mind struggles to change the subject. Recalling Freud's theories about the constant interplay between the id, the ego, and the superego, Rubião's whimsically depicted but deadly serious psychological battle in the opening two chapters of the novel sets the stage for everything that follows, for his tragic downfall.

Machado's seventh novel, *Dom Casmurro* (1900), is not only, as Helen Caldwell says, "the culmination of the six that preceded it," it is Machado's most nearly perfect single novel and one of the greatest of its time.[20] A masterpiece of psychological portraiture, of ironic inversion, and of symbolically charged narrative, *Dom Casmurro* is a towering human tragedy. With its plot structure paralleling that of *Othello, Dom Casmurro* returns once again to the use of a keenly self-conscious narrator/protagonist, whose powerful but not immediately apparent bias in regard to his telling of the story gradually emerges as the novel's great clandestine theme. Consumed, even as a callow young man, with insecurity, envy, and jealousy, the bitter old man, Dom Casmurro, who actually narrates the story, does so, one feels (recalling Freud's "talking cure"), in order to expiate the guilt that gnaws at him but that he cannot—or will not—openly acknowledge. He believes, at least on one level of his conscious mind, that he was the victim of an adulterous affair between his strong-willed wife, the enigmatic Capitú, and his best friend, Escobar. His response to what he thinks is his discovery of this infidelity is to applaud the death of his erstwhile friend, to drive his wife and child into foreign exile, and finally to wish that the child (whose biologic father he believes he is not) die of leprosy. Dom Casmurro's discourse, which constitutes the text of the novel, *Dom Casmurro,* reflects his psychoanalytically arcane and duplicitously self-serving attempt to come to grips with the possibility that he may have been wrong about the alleged affair and that it was actually he who wronged the others, all of whom are dead, more or less victims of his unyielding ferocity, and not they who wronged him. Confronted in his mind with this terrible possibility, one that is so devastating in its dark and bloody implications for him that he cannot face it openly, Dom Casmurro sets out to palliate his conscience by telling a story that, read in one way (sympathetic to Dom Casmurro), seems to substantiate what he wants to believe happened. Early in the novel, Dom Casmurro, utilizing what will become a key image, makes his ostensible purpose known: "My purpose was to tie together the two ends of my life, to restore adolescence in old age. Well, sir, I did not succeed. . . . A man consoles himself more or less for those he has lost, but I myself am missing, and this lack is essential" (5). As in *Philosopher or Dog?,* Machado here subtly integrates into an early explanatory statement the germ of the tragedy that unfolds in subsequent chapters. When mysteriously the narrator says, "I myself am missing," he is metaphorically suggesting that during what should have been the best, most fruitful, and loving years of his life, he allowed himself to become a cruel, implacable monster, a man whose warm, loving nature had been overwhelmed by his cold, uncaring, and self-ish side, which is fueled by fear, feelings of inadequacy, and jealousy. He struggles mightily to tell the truth, and thereby possibly alleviate some of the terrible guilt he senses is rightly his, but he is also like a lawyer (which he is) arguing his client's case (that is, his case) before a jury (a role in this novel played by the reader). As Caldwell suggests in *Machado de Assis,* Dom Casmurro is desperate to manipulate the story's telling so that even the reader—whose acquiescence to the narrator's version is demanded in chapter 148, "Well, and the Rest?" when Casmurro declares, "you will agree with me" (262)—will accept his version as valid and in so doing justify his actions.[21] As a careful consideration of the several interrelated levels of meaning makes clear, Dom Casmurro is both a tragic and pathetic figure, a man destroyed not dramatically by some external force but insidiously by self-love, jealousy, and fear. Apropos of this, Dom Casmurro says, in chapter 2: "Perhaps the act of narration would summon the illusion for me, . . . I will put on paper the memories that come crowding. In this way I will live what I have lived. . . ." (6).

The word "illusion" comes here to have a double, and ironic, meaning: on the one hand, all narration—all literature—is an "illusion" of something else, something most often thought of, since Plato and Aristotle, as a particular kind of "reality," or human existence. Yet at the same time, "illusion" here could be meant by Dom Casmurro to mean not the narrative presentation of "facts" but their deliberate falsification, the creating of the mere appearance, or "illusion," of truth. In a sense then Dom Casmurro, who might well be considered an early "boa-deconstructor,"[22] uses language both to tell the "truth" (as he wishes it to be) and simultaneously to lie intentionally to lead his readers (real and implied) to a conclusion he wants them to reach yet one he knows is contingent not upon any verifiable external "facts" but upon the various "illusions" of "factuality" that narrative language and structure can generate. It is not merely that *Dom Casmurro* is a metafictive meditation on a text that discusses its own creation, a narrative in which the text itself becomes the protagonist.[23] It emerges finally as a surprisingly complete post-structuralist treatise on the symbiotic relationship between language, truth, reality, and meaning. Indeed, *Dom Casmurro* epitomizes what Derrida, Culler, Paul de Man, J. Hillis Miller, and others consider to be the essential feature of deconstructive criticism, that a text necessarily undercuts itself, that because of the unstable, arbitrary, and mutually creative relationship between signifier and signified a text is inescapably in the process of "deconstructing itself" at the same time that thematically, structurally, and every other way it is trying to "construct itself" into an organically cohesive artistic whole.[24] Just as *Dom Casmurro* is at one and the same moment both Dom Casmurro's act of truth telling and his act of lying, so too is it a text that both "constructs itself" (with consummate artistic skill) and that "deconstructs itself" (calling not only its making into question but less obviously its own logocentric validity, its own veracity as "illusion"). It is indeed precisely through what Derrida and Culler call a text's "logocentrism" (the belief, central to Western thought, that "meaning" in language use is a stable and verifiable entity) that Dom Casmurro's discourse—one built on a logocentrism or "phallogocentrism" that is, a privileging of the male order in regard to such issues as truth, logic, thought and meaning that he labors self-consciously to defend—ironically undercuts his telling of the story. The very words he uses to defend his position eventually come to seem for the reader the most damning indictments of what he has done. Dom Casmurro's own argument, therefore, "deconstructs" itself.

Machado's two great narrators, Braz Cubas and especially Dom Casmurro, are both self-conscious "grammatologists" in the sense that Derrida uses the term; their concept of writing *(écriture)* is "creative," a fluid process involving at every step the writer's mental creation and each reader's individual interpretation, or "deconstruction," not of a static book but a living, changing text.[25] When Braz Cubas, for example, categorically denies that he is a cynic (chap. 34, "To a Sensitive Soul"), he undermines or "deconstructs" his own declaration by consistently doing things that are utterly cynical. Thus, Braz's entire narrative is a text dominated, at least on one level of reading, by a series of structuralist "binary oppositions," such as thought/action, what he says happened versus what "really" happened, and writing/speaking.

And in the more radically grammatological text of *Dom Casmurro,* Dom Casmurro, the narrator with an ulterior motive, "deconstructs" his own "logocentric" case primarily by means of what Derrida terms *différance,* or "deferral," the fact that the "meaning" generated by one's language use is not secure, stable, or verifiable, but a process whose significance depends on associations and relationships with other elements. Derrida's neologism, which stands in opposition to "logocentrism," refers to the way language use is a process of deferring meaning, of evolving it, rather than representing it. Hence, when in *Dom Casmurro*'s pivotal chapter, "The sketch and the color," the narrator looks at the child's face and believes he sees that the true father could only have been Escobar, he does not realize that this crucial moment's "meaning" has already been rendered moot, that is "deconstructively" balanced off or "deferred" by the "meaning" of a seemingly desultory utterance accepted by the narrator as true in an earlier chapter, "The portrait," in which he himself averred in regard to another portrait, that "sometimes, in life, there are these strange resemblances" (162). The key question of whether Capitú is or is not guilty of adultery is ultimately unresolvable, even if the work is interpreted as a logocentric narrative, because when closely examined, it maintains a perfectly balanced ambiguity on this point. But *Dom Casmurro* can be read more revealingly as a fluid poststructuralist "text" and not, to use Derrida's terminology, a static "book." The many unresolved and unresolvable oppositions of *Dom Casmurro* as "text," its carefully integrated moments of aporia (the points of doubt, indecision, or "undecidability" generated), show it systematically undermining itself at the same instant that its narrator is logocentrically producing a "book" he believes will tell the truth about what has happened between him, Capitú, Escobar, and the child Ezequiel.

Derrida's technique in approaching a text is, as many critics have pointed out, primarily a quest for equilibrium and completeness. By looking at such "binary oppositions" as writing versus speaking, a feature of Derrida's analytical method that is of special utility in *Dom Casmurro,* the reader becomes aware of the dialectical struggle, framed variously in terms of good versus evil, love versus self-love, male versus female, truth versus falsity, or life versus death, that rages within the protagonist's mind.[26] Although Dom Casmurro's "casuistic" arguments make it seem that the truth-seeking reader must agree with him, as he demands (chap. 148), a deconstructive reading of his discourse reveals the "slips" that he inadvertently makes, the small errors or inconsistencies (the points of aporia) that when considered in total suggest that quite another conclusion could be reached about who is guilty of what in this narrative. Thus, a deconstructive reading of *Dom Casmurro* can be of considerable use to us in establishing the text's true balance and completeness; indeed, in terms of our ability to know with absolute certainty who has done what to whom, *Dom Casmurro* generates through its own masterful telling an all-consuming ambiguity, one deriving not merely from some doubt as to what "really happened," but from the duplicity of language itself. Dom Casmurro picks his words carefully, believing confidently that he controls them, but the reader begins to wonder, is it not his own language, demonstrating what Fish, Derrida, and Culler call language's inevitable "slippage," that betrays him, that expresses both more and less than he wants it to? If so, *Dom Casmurro* can be read as a 1900 example not just of a text that can be read deconstructively, for any text can be so interpreted, but as the prototype of the text entirely conceived and structured around certain authorial attitudes concerning the unstable relation of language to reality and "truth" that we now associate with the critical term *deconstruction*.

A final point about *Dom Casmurro* is that it does not generate the nihilism often said to be the fatal flaw of deconstructionist criticism.[27] Among the leading deconstructionist critics, it is the humanistically inclined Miller who in "The Critic as Host" upholds deconstruction as a valid and fertile exegetical method, one that in recognizing the "pluralism" of its own methodologies avoids the nihilism, sterility, and "emptiness"[28] that some see in deconstruction, as well as in many of Machado's texts. Miller's more spacious and flexible deconstructive methods can be used profitably to explicate the intricacies and deliberate ambiguities of a text like *Dom Casmurro* and still affirm the powerfully life-affirming ethic that emanates, albeit indirectly, from it. The effect of *Dom Casmurro* is as I have said, that of a great human tragedy, one in which an otherwise good man is brought down by destructive forces within his own mind and spirit, forces he fails to control even though he would like his reader to believe that he does—this inconsistency, or "slippage," constituting yet another of the structural "binary oppositions" that make up Dom Casmurro's text. Machado's position then, similar to that advanced by Geoffrey Hartman in *Criticism in the Wilderness* (1980), was that while language might deconstructively determine our being, our ontology, this does not necessarily mean the death of the human subject and voice. Even given the apparent linguistic truths of deconstructive exegesis, literature does not have to be nonreferential, nihilistic, and depersonalized. Whether we interpret Dom Casmurro as victim (as he wishes us to do) or as the perpetrator of crimes (this distinction being perhaps the most important binary opposition of all), no reasonable person will wish to emulate him. To the contrary, the reader, horrified by what has happened (to him or caused by him), will think about how to avoid ending up like Dom Casmurro, and in making this choice the reader is led away from the nihilism of not only Casmurro but of Braz Cubas and a number of other of Machado's characters as well.

The relation between the narrator of *Dom Casmurro,* who believes that his words, his signifiers, have stable and verifiable signifieds, or meanings, and the reader, who must react to what the narrator "says," also parallels the distinction between "grammar" (a stable system of signs and meanings) and "rhetoric" (the process of reading or interpreting signs individually and collectively) that de Man establishes in *Allegories of Reading.*[29] De Man too believes that deconstruction is an appropriate approach to the "rhetorical" problems that are generated by texts like *Dom Casmurro* because rhetoric, as he defines it, requires the active presence of an interpreter in the decoding of the signs, this being the basis of the relationship between Dom Casmurro, his narrative, and the reader. Moreover, what de Man achieves in his reading of Proust's *Swann's Way*, the idea that Proust develops Swann's "reality" and his narrative by means of an interlacing of metaphor and metonymy (especially synecdoche), has implications for what Machado achieves in *Dom Casmurro*. In chapter 132, "The sketch and the color," Machado like Proust makes use of the strategies of both metaphor and metonymy to establish the multiple dimensions of this decisive chapter. Although the chapter's textual basis is that of a metaphor, the "rough sketch" that an author (time) elaborates little by little, the plot (or semantic) significance of this crucial image is developed metonymically, with the narrator's consciousness creating a meaning for and from it by letting his apprehension of the boy's eyes lead him to one of his face, his body, his entire person: "Not only his eyes, but the remaining features also, face, body, the entire person, were acquiring definition with the passage of time. They were like a rough sketch that the artist elaborates little by little. The figure begins to look out at you, smile, throb with life. . . . Escobar emerged from the grave. . ." (238–39).

Machado, like Proust, Joyce, and Mann, creates through the text created by his narrator, a metaphoric and metonymic web of multiple and perhaps endless interpretational possibilities. One can see both the logic and the utility of the position taken by E. D. Hirsch, Jr., and Gledson that a text has a single permanent meaning, the one its author intended it to have, and that a text's relevance, the result of a critical act based on interpretation, may well vary from age to age and even reader to reader.[30] Their view does not, however, negate the value of reading Dom Casmurro's text deconstructively. While we can never know in any perfect sense what single meaning Machado meant *Dom Casmurro* to have (if indeed he did intend it to have only a single meaning), we can see clearly that Dom Casmurro's would-be logocentric discourse (as opposed to the "book" he is writing, *Dom Casmurro*) amounts to a ceaseless, perfectly poised, and utterly ambiguous process of self-contradiction, "undecidability," and self-destruction. One might well argue in fact that *Dom Casmurro,* one of the earliest novels in Western literature not merely to be amenable to deconstructionism but a narrative consciously and meticulously structured entirely around its basic principles, offers an early prototype of what a deconstructively driven text would be like.

A novel written much less in the deconstructive mode, *Esau and Jacob* (1904) is nevertheless a very subtle and allegorical work in which the functioning of the narrative process emerges, as in the earlier novels, as a primary factor. An elaborately allusive, symbolic, and mythic novel, *Esau and Jacob* focuses on two interrelated relationships: one between two biologically identical but politically opposite twins, Pedro (representing the conservative past) and Paulo (representing the liberal future), and the other between these same twins and Flora, the vital present whose love for them both symbolizes the redeeming power of love and the grace, harmony, and beauty of Brazil's republic. Although the novel's title conveys a clear biblical allusion, it is Dante's symbolic use of the Esau and Jacob story that had the greatest influence on Machado's work.[31] Additionally, as in *Dom Casmurro* and *Epitaph of a Small Winner*, time figures as a major player in *Esau and Jacob*. In dealing extensively with profound political and social change in Brazil, *Esau and Jacob* shows the effect the passage of time has on all things, including social institutions. As both a knowing narrator (speaking in an omniscient third-person voice) and a contemplative one, the diplomat Ayres is the decisive character in the novel; his presentation of the story provides the attentive reader with the clues necessary to decode it. As in *Epitaph of a Small Winner* and *Dom Casmurro*, Machado's most narratively experimental novels, *Esau and Jacob*, the most symbolic and mythic of his works, demands the reader's active participation. Indeed, if the reader does not do as he or she is instructed to do, the novel's full range of philosophic and political implications can easily be missed.[32] *Esau and Jacob* opens, for example, with an image that comically evokes a memory of Dante's mountain of repentance[33] and that, as in the openings of *Dom Casmurro* and *Philosopher or Dog?*, symbolically summarizes all the conflicts that follow: "All oracles are double-tongued, but they are understood. Natividade understood the cabocla. . . . To learn that the things fated to be would be fine, and her sons great and glorious, was enough to make her happy. . . . It was . . . more than the equivalent, of Croesus' rich offerings to the Pythia."[34]

When Flora, whom Machado parallels with Dante's Beatrice, later dies, the idealism that empowered the republic seems to die as well. The twins, political enemies, both mourn her loss, implying that Brazilians of all political persuasions could legitimately mourn the passing of the republic. Although Pedro and Paulo both subsequently become deputies in their respective parties, the narrative, through Ayres's speculations, suggests that they will continue to fight each other into the future. This complex and often overlooked major novel thus ends on what at first glance seems a note of contentiousness and despair. On closer observation, however, Ayres's character also conveys a subtle sense of hope for a better, more humane, and less factionalized future, one symbolized by his wearing of a fresh, new flower (a play on the name Flora, "flor" being flower in Portuguese) in his lapel. Once again then we have evidence that for all the real Machado de Assis bitterly understood the destructiveness of time and the futility of all human endeavor, he also understood that, fail though we may, we must never cease to try to live better lives and, through these, seek a better, more just world.

Machado's final novel, *Counselor Ayres' Memorial* (1908), is in many ways a sequel to its immediate predecessor. Another socially conscious work in that the abolition of slavery in Brazil (accomplished in 1888, one year before the republic was proclaimed) plays a prominent role, *Counselor Ayres' Memorial* is also, as Nunes suggests, a subtle and sophisticated commentary on the narrative process itself, specifically, the craft of the novel as art form.[35] This final novel continues Machado's lifelong concern over the disastrous consequences of living a life based on egoism, or self-love, rather than on love of another person. Here, however, inversely recalling Felix's self-induced undoing in *Ressurreição,* love is equated with the vitality of life itself and presented, memorably in the loving devotion of the elderly couple Aguiar and Carmo, as the only human force able to overcome the ravages of time; though time can wither our bodies, it cannot—if we choose not to let it—wither the love we feel for someone else. Indeed, as Aguiar and Carmo so movingly illustrate, the passage of time may make our love grow ever stronger, transcending, finally even death itself. Love, Machado suggests in this elegiac final novel, is—for those who choose it and work to keep its flame alive—the ultimate victory of human existence over the destructiveness of time. The novel is at least partly autobiographical because in letters to friends Machado definitely identified his deceased wife, Carolina, with Aguiar's wife, Carmo.[36] Also interesting, as Caldwell notes, is that in the original manuscript of the novel, written entirely in Machado's own hand, the names of the two female characters, the aged Carmo and the youthful Fidelia, were constantly written in one for the other, then crossed out and changed back again. Caldwell interprets this to mean that for Machado, both Carmo and Fidelia are portraits of his wife: Fidelia is the young Carolina, Carmo the old.[37] A sad if beautiful paean to the absolute need for unselfish and unstinting love in human affairs, *Counselor Ayres' Memorial,* though slight in size, is great in its poignantly lyrical presentation of this most fundamental of Machado's themes.

Chapter Six
The Short Story Collections

For all Machado's innovative skill and imagination as a novelist, many critics, including Lúcia Miguel Pereira, Renard Pérez, and Barreto Filho, believe he attained his highest levels of excellence in the demanding short story form, a genre Machado cultivated throughout his career. His first published story, a comic piece about mistaken identity and a spurious love affair involving the narrator's wife and best friend entitled, "Três tesouros perdidos" (Three lost treasures), appeared 5 January 1858, when he was eighteen years old.[1] In all, Machado wrote more than two hundred pieces of short fiction, many of which originally appeared in literary journals and were anthologized much later; some have been discovered only very recently.[2] During Machado's lifetime, seven collections of stories, a few of which had appeared earlier in journals, were published. Other stories have appeared posthumously, as in *Outros contos* and *Outras relíquias,* reflecting Machado's enduring popularity in Brazil and reinforcing his reputation as the father of the modern Brazilian short story.[3]

Technically and thematically, the history of Machado's development as a story writer parallels his development as a novelist. Like the novels the stories reflect an even higher level of technical sophistication and a steady movement away from romanticism, often rendered ironically, toward a subtle and complex mixture of psychological realism and symbolism.

Even in the early works, however, several features characteristic of the Machadoan short story stand out. According to Mário Matos, Machado's stories are typically urban rather than rural; they depict characters in the process of thinking and feeling rather than in action; they are orally oriented (creating the impression that the reader is hearing them rather than reading them); they feature a great deal of psychologically self-revealing dialogue and monologue as opposed to description or narration; they are told from either an epic perspective (in which they are seen to represent certain social types, traits, or problems) or a dramatic one (in which the characters reveal themselves, this being Machado's most effective and predilect manner of presentation); they often involve antithesis, irony, and surprise, or unexpected themes, revelations, and turns of events; they often lack conventional plots and instead focus on imagistically rendered revelations of character or theme; they show a strong enthusiasm for the creation of enigmatic female characters (both as protagonists and as secondary characters); they reflect an ironic or bittersweet sense of life as a tragicomic affair; they are nearly always humorous (genteelly so in the early works but, as in the novels, more mordantly, resignedly, or "pessimistically" so in the later works); they are critically self-conscious about their artifice and metafictively flout the nature of the truth they present; they are full of characters—men more than women (undoubtedly a reflection of Machado's realization that few positions of social power or authority were open to women)—who epitomize certain Brazilian social types, institutions, or conditions of their age; they develop the sea as a virtual motif of the author's work; they are full of philosophic and often sharply ironic aphorisms about life (many of which reappear throughout his work). The stories repeat Machado's basic corpus of themes: the destructiveness of time, humanity's temporally limited existence, the problems caused by our vanity, doubt, and selfishness, our frustrating inability to attain in life the state of perfection we conceive in our mind, the nature of madness, and our enthusiasm for seeking the solutions to our problems in external sources, such as science or institutionalized religion, rather than in our own need to choose between what is right and wrong (symbolized everywhere in Machado's work by the choice between love of self, or selfishness, and love of others).[4] As Machado matured these basic characteristics gained in sophistication.

From a critical perspective, it is useful to consider Machado's first two story collections, *Contos fluminenses* (1869) and *Histórias da meia-noite* (1873), as a single unit. With only a few exceptions, such as the psychologically oriented "Miss Dollar," Ernesto de tal," and "Linha reta e linha curva" (Straight line and curved line) or "O relógio de ouro" (The gold watch), "A parasita azul" (The blue parasite), and "Ponto de vista" (Point of view), respectively, the stories of these first two collections are well written but otherwise rather undistinguished. "Miss Dollar," for example, an ironic and self-conscious story with a surprise revelation ("Miss Dollar" turns out to be a remarkable dog), deals with the issue of how language shapes and determines our readerly expectations in ways not immediately apparent to us. While one can in such titles as "Straight Line and Curved Line" and "The Gold Watch" (which is one of the best stories overall in the two collections) already see a tendency toward metaphorically driven narratives, the majority of these early pieces deal in various ways with the kinds of domestic parlor intrigues, including adultery, we associate with romanticism. Moreover, with the exceptions noted above, these overly long and occasionally tedious early pieces do not show the same concision and economy of means so brilliantly employed in the later works.

Like Machado's novels his stories can be divided up into early and late periods. The first of the later or mature story collections is *Papéis avulsos,* which appeared in 1882, one year after *Epitaph of a Small Winner* came out in book form. Like the novel the pieces in *Papéis avulsos* show dramatic changes in theme, form, and technique. From the late 1870s on Machado, increasingly committed to narrative, published stories that amounted to a sharp and satirically perspicacious assault on the otiose middle-class values and social structures of Brazil's Second Empire (1840–90) and the early years of the republic (established in 1889). As Jack Schmitt and Lorie Ishimatsu observe of the stories that make up *Papéis avulsos* and later works: "There is an abundance of implicit social criticism in Machado's descriptions of the life styles and the family structures of middle-class characters in his stories. One is always aware that the material comforts his characters enjoy are either the fruits of a carefully observed caste system or achieved at the expense of others."[5]

One of the most famous of the narratives included in *Papéis avulsos* is "The Psychiatrist," an extended tale that satirizes the tendency to seek in science, or in the name of science, solutions to human defects. Read on its most superficial level, "The Psychiatrist" addresses the twin questions of who in this life is insane (as opposed to who is not) and how can we tell? Read deconstructively, the story centers squarely on the impossibility of knowing for certain what the word *insane* means and therefore what it means to be insane. Structurally, as in *Dom Casmurro* and James's *Ambassadors,* the story involves an ironic inversion of roles: Dr. Simão Bacamarte, the learned protagonist for whom science is the only truth, begins the story by rather sanctimoniously committing other people to an insane asylum known as the "Green House"; later, he ends it by judging these formerly insane people to be sane and committing himself. Thus the story's basic binary opposition, sanity versus insanity, is coupled with the larger epistemological problem of meaning and knowledge, with the relationship between language and existence, and our cognition of both. Since even science is forced to use language, an imprecise and ever evolving human invention to define and delineate "madness" in a person, it too proves a failure in its attempt to eliminate ambiguity, uncertainty, and contradiction from our understanding of the human condition. Bacamarte's initial definition of insanity is so comprehensive in its applicability that nearly every "normal" person can be rationally defined as "crazy," an idea echoed in many other of Machado's works when "normal," "sane" people like Felix, Braz Cubas, or Dom Casmurro consciously choose to conduct their lives in "abnormal" or "insane" ways.

Later in the story, however, Bacamarte's initial position which he developed logically and "scientifically," showing the unquestioning confidence of a zealot, is totally reversed by Bacamarte himself, who, without ever wondering about the validity of what he is doing, blithely creates a new theory of insanity in which the "sick" (formerly the well) are, absurdly, considered the "rational." As the story's narrative voice explains, "The psychiatrist informed the Council . . . that as a consequence of this reexamination in the light of the statistics, he had concluded not only that his theory was unsound but also that the exactly contrary doctrine was true—that is, that normality lay in a lack of equilibrium and that the abnormal, the really sick, were the well balanced, the thoroughly rational. . . ."[6] Ludicrously undisturbed by this sudden reversal of positions, Bacamarte, a rational paragon, eventually begins to wonder about his theory, however. Upon releasing as "cured" all the asylum's inmates, he muses to himself, "Were they all really insane? Did I really cure them? Or is not mental imbalance so natural and inherent that it was bound to assert itself with or without my help?" (43).

After "twenty minutes" of "rational" inquiry, Bacamarte discovers—in himself—the one "undeniably well balanced, virtuous, insane man" he sought, the one who "possessed wisdom, patience, tolerance, truthfulness, loyalty, and moral fortitude—all the qualities that go to make an utter madman" (44). Declaring that his newest "discovery" "is a matter of science, of a new doctrine" and that he embodies both its theory and practice, Bacamarte, "his eyes alight with scientific conviction, . . . set about the business of curing himself" (44). Wryly, the omniscient narrator remarks that some of his former "patients" had ventured to suggest that, given his demise, the good doctor, "was the only madman . . . ever committed to the asylum" (44).

Possibly inspired, as Gomes suggests, by Machado's reading of Swift's *Serious and Useful Scheme to Make a Hospital for Incurables,*[7] "The Psychiatrist," one of the first great stories from Machado's "mature" period, is a comic masterpiece of satire and ironic inversion that, through its deliberate exposition of the arbitrary semantic codes that operate between signifier and signified, human existence and our urge to find meaning in it involves the basic precepts not only of structuralist literary analysis but those of poststructuralism as well. Along with "The Looking Glass," "The Bonzo's Secret," "The Education of a Stuffed Shirt," and "Final Request," "The Psychiatrist" numbers among Machado's most accomplished stories.[8]

Machado's next collection of stories, *Histórias sem data* (1884), continues the artistic growth so dramatically begun in *Papéis avulsos.* Outstanding stories like "The Devil's Church," "Final Chapter," "A Strange Thing," "Alexandrian Tale," "Plus Ultra!" "Those Cousins from Sapucaia," "A Second

Life," and "Admiral's Night"[9] all reflect Machado's increasingly ironic world view, his pungent humor, his technical experimentations with point of view and structuring, and his ever more subtle use of symbolism and imagery to advance his plot structures. As is evident in these compact, concentrated stories, Machado was mastering the genial but laconic style that marked his greatest works. Striking for its sharply ironic drollery as well as for its exceptional economy of expression, "Alexandrian Tale" is like "The Psychiatrist" a satirical assault on the tendency to seek science (or any other external source) as a panacea for human problems, which, Machado's texts imply, can only be solved by individuals making choices that lead to moral rather than immoral lives. This powerful but subdued sense of the need for moral human conduct permeates Machado's work and, in addition to offsetting the charge that Machado is a bleakly nihilistic writer, also constitutes the mechanism by which Machado philosophically endows his characters with both a universal significance and a particular social or cultural dimension. Machado's basic method is to show the reader what he considers to be the truth concerning the human condition, the propensity to do evil (generally associated with egoism and selfishness), the illusory nature of truth, the transitoriness of life, and the endless hypocrisies upon which individual lives and entire societies are built, and then leave the reader, who has been actively drawn into the texts, to make his or her own decisions about how to act, about how to live.

A unique feature of "Alexandrian Tale," however, is its sadism. Perpetrated in the name of science against helpless and innocent victims, first rats and then humans, the sadistic violence done to living things by those who believe they are going to save the human race is trenchantly contrasted to the serenity and sanctimoniousness with which its agents perform it: "Science, like war, has its imperious necessities. . . . Stroibus caged the rats and subjected them to the knife one by one. A less skillful surgeon would have frequently interrupted the procedure because the victims' spasms of pain and agony made the handling of the scalpel awkward. . . . But this was precisely Stroibus' superiority: he possessed the trained unflinching self-assuredness of a master surgeon.

At Stroibus' side, Pythias collected the blood and assisted with the operations, restraining the patients' convulsive movements and observing the progress of the agony in the animals' eyes."[10] Though not frequently employed in his work, violence does appear from time to time in Machado's work. Generally its effect is to subtly remind us that, far from being benign or irrelevant, the actions we choose to take in life can under certain circumstances have direct physical consequences for other people. In addition, however, to underscoring the importance of making moral choices in life,

Machado's use of violence also reminds us that we live in an absurd universe, one utterly indifferent to our fate and our conduct and one in which good and evil, like love and self-love, coexist simultaneously, with each one exerting a strong if contradictory influence on our thoughts and actions.

Physical violence also plays a role in "The Companion," one of the several excellent stories in Machado's fifth anthology. *Várias histórias* (1896). Allowing modestly in his introduction that the short narratives of *Várias histórias* are "inferior" to those of Prosper Mérimée and Edgar Allan Poe (whose stories he believes to be among the best written in America), Machado with characteristic wit also avers that even his "poor" pieces have one great advantage over novels: they are short.

The brevity of the stories in *Várias histórias,* however, also demonstrates how economical Machado had become in his writing. Epitomizing Flaubert's passion for finding "the precise word," Machado shows here that he has mastered the art of making a few words do the work of many. Indeed, it is precisely from this exceptional economy of means that Machado generates the ambiguity and complexity that critics like Meyer, Caldwell and Nunes find so characteristic of his work. By building "texts" (in Derrida's sense of the term) that develop through a concise, often ironic and "minimalist" prose style and that structure themselves around certain often recurring images, motifs, and symbols, Machado's artfully controlled ambiguity is never in any sense that of a confused or uncertain story. Rather, it is the complex and dynamic relativism of stories that, involving both the author's intention (or intentions) and each reader's response to the text, open themselves up in an endless process of reader involvement and interpretation. Commenting on Machado's famous ambiguity, Schmitt and Ishimatsu observe that "by aiming at psychological truth and focusing on crucial moments of experience in the lives of his characters, he approaches the method of the moderns. His ambiguity is in part the result of his subjective, relativistic world view, in which truth and reality, which are never absolutes, can only be approximated; no character relationships are stable, no issues are clear-cut, and the nature of everything is tenuous."[11] This intentionally generated and artistically maintained ambiguity is consistently present in such ironically charged stories as "A Woman's Arms," "A Celebrity," "The Secret Heart," "Adam and Eve," "The Companion," "The Diplomat," "Mariana," "Dona Paula," "Life," and "The Fortune-Teller," works that give ample evidence why Machado, along with de Maupassant, Chekhov, and James, deserves recognition as one of the true masters of the modern short story form.[12]

"The Companion" continues to be one of Machado's most anthologized pieces. An ironic, darkly comic tale of violence, greed, and the self-serving

human balm of rationalization, "The Companion" tells the story of a man
hired as a nurse for an irascible and malicious old invalid, a man so conten-
tious and cantankerous that he drives his companion to murder him. The
story's narrator, the man who has committed the crime, delivers his story to
the reader in a fully self-conscious, metaphoric, and macabrely comic mode:
"So you think what happened to me in 1860 could be put in a book? . . .
Look, I could even tell you my whole life story—it has other points of interest
. . . read this and wish me well. Forgive whatever appears evil to you, and
don't be surprised if what I have to say gives off an odor quite distinct from
that of a rose. You asked me for a human document, and here it is."[13] The
story ends ironically with the murderer not only never accused of having committed a crime but actually inheriting his victim's fortune. In addition, he is
widely venerated by people who in a moment of sharp dramatic irony praise
him for the "Christian patience," "loyalty," and "devotion" with which he had
served the old man. The reader, however, who unlike the other characters
knows what really happened, also gets to observe how the narrator's progressive self-delusion about what he did begins to move him from speaking
about the murder he committed to calling it at the story's conclusion an "ac-
cident" (84), one that in a surprising turnabout had left him quite wealthy,
the legal beneficiary of the man he murdered. Thus, the human penchant for
self-delusion becomes a major thematic force in the story, one reinforced by
the sense of moral obtuseness shown by the narrator and his reaction to the
events he describes.

Another story that brilliantly represents Machado's ability to create and
sustain an ambiguous fictive world is "Midnight Mass," the centerpiece of his
sixth collection of stories, *Páginas recolhidas,* published in 1899 and often
said to be Machado's finest overall story collection. Widely judged to be
Machado's greatest single story, "Midnight Mass" is a masterpiece of repressed sexuality, of psychological insight, and atmospheric ambiguity. The
story's basic plot involves what may or may not have been the sexual attraction between a young man, who is telling the story in retrospect, and a young
married woman, Conceição. At the outset of the story, the narrator openly
admits to his own "confusion" surrounding the events he will relate: "I have
never quite understood a conversation that I had with a lady many years ago,
when I was seventeen and she was thirty. It was Christmas Eve. I had arranged
to go to Mass with a neighbor and was to rouse him at midnight for this
purpose."[14] The narrator, who, saying he lived quietly with his books in a
room of the house owned by the lady in question and her husband, subtly establishes (or seeks to establish) his innocence and naiveté in matters of male
and female relationships. Yet because the narrator also notes that at one point

he learned both that the man Menezes was having an affair and that seemingly his wife, Conceição, not only knew of the affair but gradually came to accept it as "proper," it is possible to view him as less "innocent" than he would have the reader believe. Indeed, one very plausible reader response to his particular manner of presenting these facts is to speculate whether the narrator perhaps sensed that he and a "neglected" young wife living in such close quarters might develop a relationship from which a tryst could emerge. With his mind perhaps unconsciously cogitating on these ideas, the narrator intriguingly describes the woman: "Gentle Conceição! They called her the saint and she merited the title, so uncomplainingly did she suffer her husband's neglect. . . . Everything about her was passive and attenuated. . . . She spoke ill of no one, she pardoned everything. She didn't know how to hate; quite possibly she didn't know how to love" (94–95). By having already suggested that Conceição not only knew about but accepted her husband's infidelity, and by suggesting that she may not have known "how to love," the narrator intentionally or not continues to imply simultaneously that he was merely the detached observer of this entire scenario and that, sensing an opportunity for a sexual liaison, he could "teach" a frustrated woman—who, knowing herself to be the victim of an unfaithful husband, might well be receptive to the idea of seeking sexual fulfillment elsewhere—"how to love." The ambiguity of the story's presentation and interpretation is perfectly poised and maintained right through to the conclusion.

The story's repressed sexual tension is heightened when, after reading for a time the highly romantic Three Musketeers (which could easily have erotically stimulated the narrator's mind), he suddenly sees Conceição enter the room where he is reading. All alone late at night, Conceição, who, he learns, has not slept at all (possibly, one speculates, because of her sexual frustrations), and the narrator begin to chat. The narrator's description of Conceição's dramatic entrance (coming perhaps strategically after her mother had gone to bed) is crucial to the reader's interpretation of what is happening, an interpretation that may be at variance with what the narrator implies, or wishes to imply: "After a time, however, a sound from the interior of the house roused me from my book. . . . I raised my head. Soon I saw the form of Conceição appear at the door . . . Conceição, wearing her bedroom slippers, came into the room. She was dressed in a white negligee, loosely bound at the waist. Her slenderness helped to suggest a romantic apparition quite in keeping with the spirit of my novel. . . . She sat on the chair facing mine, near the sofa. . . . Her eyes were not those of a person who had just slept . . ." (95).

Dressed in this fashion, with a loosely bound negligee, Conceição leans forward, ostensibly to "hear better," and crosses her legs, all acts or circumstances that could be interpreted as being either deliberately seductive or as being merely very casual, domestic, and even familial in nature. Suggesting, however, that she is struggling with a conflict between an expression of her frustrated sexuality and her religious views (that sex is sinful), Conceição initiates a series of surprising comments about what she takes to be the salacious nature of two pictures (one of which is of Cleopatra) hung in the room:

". . . to tell the truth, I'd prefer pictures of saints. These are better for bachelors' quarters or a barber shop."
"A barber shop! I didn't think you'd ever been to . . ."
"But I can imagine what the customers there talk about while they're waiting—girls and flirtations, and naturally the proprietor wants to please them with pictures they'll like. But I think pictures like that don't belong in the home. That's what I think, but I have a lot of queer ideas." (99)

Intimating that he himself was not certain what he wanted to have happen, the narrator then observes, of his own response to Conceição's apparel, conduct, and words: "I wished and I did not wish to end the conversation. I tried to take my eyes from her, and did so out of respect; but, afraid she would think I was tired of looking at her, when in truth I was not, I turned again towards her" (100).

At this point the story abruptly begins to come to a close. Conceição and the narrator, enveloped (as the narrator presents it) in a dreamlike reverie, fall silent. A friend of the narrator then appears, rapping on the window to call the narrator off to Midnight Mass. In a deliciously ambiguous moment of plurisignation, one charged with two levels of meaning (one denotatively literal and the other sensually connotative), Conceição observes, "Hurry, hurry, don't make him wait. It was my fault. Good-bye until tomorrow" (100).[15] The ambiguity inherent under these circumstances in the words "don't make him wait" implies both that Conceição is referring to the person at the window and, allowing for a pronominal change (one perhaps already existing in Conceição's agitated mind) from "him" to "me," to herself. From this, one could then infer that when Conceição says "It was my fault" she is speaking both to the man at the window (whom she does not wish to keep waiting) and to her own repressed sexuality, a confused manifestation of which the genesis of the entire episode may have been.

As in the case of *Dom Casmurro,* which appeared six years later, "Midnight Mass" is not simply ambiguous; it is a story meticulously structured around the inherently ambiguous nature of language, around the unresolved conflicts or "slippages" between logocentric signifieds and the ever unstable and often contradictory signifiers. Establishing a final opposition between the events (real and imagined) of a "romantic" night and those of a "realistic" day, between religion and sensuality, between life and death, and most importantly between the narrator and Conceição, the story draws to its uncertain but artistically perfect conclusion:

> And with her rocking gait Conceição walked softly down the hall. . . . During Mass, Conceição kept appearing between me and the priest; charge this to my seventeen years. Next morning at breakfast I spoke of the midnight Mass and of the people I had seen in church, without, however, exciting Conceição's interest. During the day I found her, as always, natural, benign, with nothing to suggest the conversation of the prior evening.
> A few days later I went to Mangaratiba. When I returned to Rio in March, I learned that the notary had died of apoplexy. . . . I learned later that she had married her husband's apprenticed clerk.
>
> (100)

The story's last line provides one final tantalizing bit of information. Read one way, the fact that upon her husband's death Conceição had married his "apprentice clerk" could easily be taken as yet one more objective piece of reportage about this entire episode. Read another way, however, it could suggest either that Conceição was already having an affair with the clerk or, frustrated as she was (or thought to be), that she had indeed all along been seeking some form of sexual experience, either with the clerk or with the narrator of the story. The story's essential ambiguity then is really twofold: the narrator's "confusion" about what took place and, more importantly, Conceição's confusion over how to proceed given her husband's infidelity and her own sexual needs.

Machado's seventh collection of stories, *Relíquias de casa velha* (1906), which opens with an elegiac sonnet, "A Carolina," to his beloved and recently deceased wife, Carolina, was the last of his story anthologies to be published before his death in 1908. This final collection contains a number of stories that show Machado's continuing mastery of the short narrative form. Pungently ironic and psychologically compelling yet possessed of a keen social consciousness, stories like "Father versus Mother," "Funeral March," "The Holiday," "Evolution," and "Pylades and Orestes" experiment modernistically with time, with various types of fallible, self-conscious narrators, and with differing manners of character presentation and plot development. Intensely synecdochic and metaphoric, these wryly comic and compact tales are, like those of Joyce's *Dubliners* (1914), exercises in the artistic integration of the modes of both realism and symbolism. In terms of their structuring, their acute awareness of time's destructive passing, and their advancement of plot by symbolic and allusive means, stories like "Funeral March," "Evolution," and "Father versus Mother" (to say nothing of "Midnight Mass") compare favorably with such Joycean classics as "Araby," "Clay," and "The Dead."

A final collection of stories, *Outros contos,* was published posthumously. The tales in this collection, notable among which are "Mariana," "The Animal Game," and "Casa velha" (The old house), were culled by critics from among those pieces that Machado had not included in his previous volumes.[16] Ranging in date of publication from 1864 ("Virgínius: narrativa de um advogado"; Virgínius: the narrative of an attorney) to 1906 ("Um incêndio"; A fire), these stories, most of which have not been translated, demonstrate in dramatic fashion Machado's continuing artistic growth and development as a writer of short narratives. Especially notable in this regard is the rather longish story "Casa velha," which, appearing between 1885 and 1886, is sometimes considered Machado's tenth novel.

In general, Machado's post-1873 stories exemplify the same technical expertise, innovativeness, and psychological nuance that we associate with such better-known masters of the modern short story form as James, Poe, Chekhov, Mérimée, de Maupassant, Woolf, Kafka, and Joyce. Like James Machado found the necessarily compressed form of the short story an ideal genre in which to work and like de Maupassant he learned to present his observations accurately and without obvious moral judgments. An early pioneer in the area of dramatic characterization, that is, the process of allowing characters to reveal themselves rather than being described, Machado de Assis was also an innovator in his many experiments with self-conscious narrators and metafictional texts. His technical expertise is also apparent in his innovative implementation of a condensed, oral, and imagistic style, and in his predilection for developing tragicomic conflicts of a psychological or philosophic nature that, through the character types that express them, nevertheless generate a sharply critical social consciousness. In this regard one thinks of de Maupassant, Woolf, and Joyce, though several other modern masters could be cited as well. Machado's two most singular stylistic features, his development of plot through a closely interwoven web of symbols, images, metaphors, and in the manner of Eliot and Joyce often ironic allusions, and his Flaubert-like economy of expression, are more strikingly evident in his short narratives than in his novels. But whether we consider him primarily as a short story writer or as a novelist, Machado de Assis deserves—and is beginning to receive—recognition as one of the true modern masters of Western narrative.

Chapter Seven
The Poetry

Although Machado wrote verse throughout his career, poetry was not a genre in which he achieved the brilliance of his fiction. Machado's development as a poet nonetheless reflects the same basic evolution away from romanticism and toward a metaphorically rendered realism that we see so clearly in his novels and short stories. Having in 1855 made his literary debut as a poet,[1] Machado went on to produce during his lifetime more than one hundred eighty original poems, twenty-five verse translations, and five imitations and paraphrases in verse.[2] Thematically, his later poems, those of *Ocidentais* (1901) in particular, deal with philosophic problems similar to those in the post-1880 narratives. Viewed as a whole, Machado's four books of poetry (*Crisálidas*, 1864; *Falenas*, 1870; *Americanas*, 1875; and *Ocidentais*, 1901) show him to have been a major figure, creatively and critically, in the rise of Brazilian parnassianism, a mode of verse composition that was the poetic equivalent of realism in narrative and that stressed objectivity, precision of detail, clarity of expression, and formal perfection.

If we cannot rank Machado as a great poet, we are able to say that in some ten or twelve poems he did achieve poetic works of true distinction.[3] From his first published poem until his last, Machado de Assis was a poet whose works, including the truly outstanding pieces, were characterized by an intellectual bent and a correctness of language and form rather than by displays of emotion or an interest in formal experimentation. Overall, critics have tended to view him as a very correct if somewhat "cold" poet, one who lacked a vivid imagination, suffered from a limited vocabulary, was indifferent to nature (nature having long been a staple of Brazilian poetry) and deficient in descriptive powers.[4] It is perhaps fitting then that Machado, whose entire career reflects a lifelong penchant for irony and antithesis, succeeded most as a poet when he was writing narrative, that is, when he was merging the modes of poetry with those of prose.

Machado's first published book of poems, *Crisálidas* (1864), shows the twenty-five-year-old author to have had a basically romantic sense of art and life. Consisting of twenty-two original poems, four translations, one "paraphrase," and one "imitation," *Crisálidas* deals with such themes as love (both our need for it and, as in "Erro" (Error), our vain perversion of it and dissatisfaction with it), the nature and function of the poet, religious faith, and social and political issues.[5] While many of these early poems are routinely romantic, others, such as "No limiar" (On the threshold), "Versos a Corina" (Verses to Corina) "Aspiração" (Aspiration), and "Tristeza" (Sadness), show a nascent sense of the disillusionment and frustration that characterize the works of the mature writer. "Versos a Corina," perhaps the best-known poem from *Crisálidas,* recounts the story of a failed love affair, for example. In *La jeunesse de Machado de Assis,* Jean-Michel Massa argues that the woman of the poem was a real person, one who had been a great love of Machado but who had rejected him perhaps because of his racial heritage.[6] Regardless, "Versos a Corina" is also noteworthy for the degree of emotional pain it expresses. It is one of the few poems in *Crisálidas* that displays a substantial amount of genuine passion, the other poems being more intellectualized and objective.

Machado's keen patriotism is evident in works like "Hino patriótico" (Patriotic hymn), a poem inspired by the so-called "Christie Affair" of 1862–63 and in which Machado praises Brazil's refusal to yield to what he and a great many other Brazilians felt was an unreasonable and unjust affront to Brazil by Great Britain.[7] This poem quickly became immensely popular in Brazil and was even set to music and performed at the Ginásio and Lírico Fluminense theaters.[8]

An extension of the progressive and sincere patriotism he felt for his native land, Machado's interest in political issues is clearly apparent in poems such as "O acordar da Polônia" (The awakening of Poland), "Epitáfio do México" (Epitaph of Mexico) and "Os arlequins" (the harlequins). Both "Epitáfio do México" (22 November 1863) and "Os arlequins" (April 1864) were recited by Machado at literary soirées, which he frequented regularly and it seems with considerable relish. The central theme of "Epitáfio do México" like that of "O acordar da Polônia" is that people who have long been under the yoke of tyranny and foreign rule will eventually rise again and win back their freedom and independence.

"No limiar" is perhaps the best single poem of *Crisálidas,* the one that for many critics is formally and thematically the most quintessentially Machadoan composition of the collection. Tightly written in terza rima, a poetic form consisting of three-line stanzas with a rhyme scheme of *a b a, b c b, c d c,* "No limiar" is one of Machado's early attempts at a metaphysical poem, one dealing with the ambivalent interplay of hope and disillusionment in the human experience. In its succinct if not subtle skepticism about the plight of human beings, "No limiar," with its negative tone and philosophic orientation, presages one of Machado's more sophisticated later sonnets, "No alto" (On high), the concluding poem of *Ocidentais*, in which not even the poet can escape life's disillusionment. In "No limiar," however, the earlier version of this maddening conflict between hope and disillusionment, it is clearly the latter that predominates over the former.

Upon its publication in 1864, *Crisálidas* elicited a mixed reaction from the critical establishment. Though many reviews were favorable, others noted the lack of originality that typified the poems, their formal simplicity, and their general paucity of emotional power. The poem "Versos a Corina" was singled out as the most appealing and engaging while the patriotic pieces were lauded for their social value, their correctness of language, and their attention to poetic form.[9] If in general the poems of *Crisálidas* show Machado to have been a rather orthodox romantic in terms of his thematics, the formal simplicity, the linguistic precision, and the clarity of the images suggest a certain inchoate predisposition toward the parnassianism that began to appear more decisively in *Falenas*, Machado's second book of poetry.

Published in 1869, *Falenas* contained thirty-five compositions, twenty-two of which were original works and thirteen of which were translations. The title *Falenas* (Moths) when considered in terms of the title of his first work, *Crisálidas* (Chrysalises), shows both that Machado, even at this early point in his career, had begun to master the use of metaphors as a method of advancing an idea and that he was quite aware of his own growth and development as a writer.[10] Divided into four sections, "Vária" (Various), "Lira chinesa" (Chinese lyre), "Uma ode de Anacreonte" (An ode of Anacreonte), and "Pálida Elvira" (Pale Elvira), *Falenas*, like *Crisálidas*, is not organized around any single thematic or structural consideration.[11] Showing once again the meticulous attention to form and language that had characterized *Crisálidas*, *Falenas* differs from the earlier work in that it makes a much greater use of the Alexandrine line, the "triolet," and the sonnet, the latter being a form Machado later mastered. Thematically, *Falenas* is on balance more positive and optimistic than *Crisálidas*, a work in which failure, frustration, and disillusionment are the dominant sentiments. While, for example, in "No limiar" (*Crisálidas*) hope had been cast in a losing role, in *Falenas* and "Musa dos olhos verdes" (The green-eyed muse) it is portrayed in a guardedly optimistic fashion as a source of possible consolation for humankind.[12] And if Machado's apparently unrequited love for Corina, so movingly expressed in "Versos a Corina," exemplifies the treatment love receives in *Crisálidas*, in *Falenas*, published after Machado had successfully courted and wed (in 1869) Carolina Xavier de Novais, introspective poems like "Sombras" (Shadows), "Quando ela fala" (When she speaks), "Noivado"

(Betrothal), "Livros e flores" (Books and flowers), and "Pássaros" (Birds) all evince a cautious yet hopeful optimism about love and its restorative powers.

If not necessarily numbering among *Falena*'s most popular compositions, the poems "Un vieux pays" (An old country), "O verme" (The worm), "Uma ode de Anacreonte," and "Pálida Elvira" are widely considered to represent the collection's highest levels of artistic achievement. Written originally in French, "Un vieux pays" moreover proves how thoroughly Machado, largely self-taught, had by 1869 mastered the French language.[13]

In addition to showing his fluent command of French, Machado's "Un vieux pays" also generates the sense of pessimism that is frequently said to typify Machado's mature works. Constructed on the principle of antithesis, which Machado exploited to perfection in later works, and reflecting the constant interplay of opposites that so fascinated him about the human condition, this poem like "No limiar" and several later ones shows "good" being continually undercut or tainted by "evil." Quite possibly influenced in its imagery and tone by Charles Baudelaire's *Fleurs du mal* (1857), "Un vieux pays" stands out as one of *Falenas*'s most singular efforts.

Another of the most interesting poems from this second collection is "O verme," a short, sixteen-line work that develops the image of a flower destroyed by a worm, anticipating its later, more subtle use in *Epitaph of a Small Winner* and *Dom Casmurro* where jealousy (the worm) gnaws away at our better instincts (the flower): "Esta flor é o coração / Aquele verme o ciúme" (This flower is the heart / that worm, jealousy).

In contrast to the rather somber and melancholy "O verme," "Uma ode de Anacreonte" shows Machado developing a vein of ironic humor. Composed of ninety-seven octaves, "Pálida Elvira" is a self-conscious metapoem whose voice often speaks directly to the reader about the poem's development. Referring to the persona of "Pálida Elvira," Ishimatsu remarks that "the speaker's frequent digressions from the main narrative, constant remarks to the reader, ironic and humorous perspective, and skepticism toward the cultural trends of his day are all signs of Machado's progressive maturation as a writer."[14] While César Leal believes that certain aspects of the form and mood of "Pálida Elvira" could reflect the direct influence of Luis de Góngora's "Fábula de Polifemo," it is equally possible, as Ishimatsu notes, that Álvares de Azevedo's "O poema do frade" could have provided the inspiration for Machado's work.[15] The poem's primary story, centering on the characters Elvira, an innocent, pale, and swooning virgin, and Heitor, a Byronic hero with a Faustian thirst for knowledge, amounts to an ironic pillorying of what Machado considered the already stale conventions of literary romanticism. By naming his main female character Elvira, and by having her possess a copy of "Le lac," Machado alludes to Alphonse de Lamartine, an influential figure in French romanticism. Satirizing the tired clichés of romantic literature, "Pálida Elvira" ends predictably with the death of Elvira and the suicide of Heitor, who, vitiated by a kind of world-weariness and romantic weltschmerz, throws himself into the sea, an act that Isaac Goldberg wryly observes "he might well have done before the poem began."[16]

The other outstanding piece in *Falenas* is "Uma ode de Anacreonte," a one-act play in verse dealing with the venerable Machadoan themes of selfishness, the betrayal of love, deception, and vanity. Written in Alexandrine couplets and featuring an unsuccessful love triangle, "Uma ode de Anacreonte," set in ancient Greece, tells rather didactically the story of Mirto, a vain and fickle young courtesan; Cleon, a poor but idealistic poet; and Lísias, a rich and materialistic merchant. Mirto, seeking a wealthy husband, inevitably comes to choose Lísias over Cleon, who at the end of the poem finds himself disillusioned by both love and friendship. Earmarked by considerable irony, cynicism, brooding reflection and resignation,[17] "Uma ode de Anacreonte" generates a tone that closely parallels that of the dour prose and poetry of the later Machado.

The critical reception of *Falenas* was similar to that accorded *Crisálidas*. Most of the reviews were positive, though a few critics judged *Falenas* mediocre, seeing it redeemed by only a few memorable poems. The one really negative review of *Falenas* came from Sílvio Romero, a positivistic and "scientifically" oriented critic who around 1870 had also begun to challenge the long reign of romanticism in Brazilian literature. Romero, who a few years later became virtually the only major Brazilian critic to disparage the works of Machado's mature phase, decried what he felt with some justification to be the "subjectivistic lyricism" of many of the pieces in the work.[18] Although *Crisálidas* is overall more typically romantic than *Falenas*, which shows a certain parnassian bent, the two works seem largely cut from the same cloth. As José Maria Belo remarks of *Crisálidas* and *Falenas*, "It does not seem to me possible to distinguish between the first two books; they obey the same inspiration and the same processes."[19] In terms of Machado's control over the various poetic techniques and forms available to him, however, *Falenas* does indicate definite growth in his artistic development.

Americanas, published in 1875, interrupted Machado's evolution away from romanticism and toward parnassianism; by dealing primarily with the concept and figure of the Brazilian, or "American," Indian, it returned thematically to one of the most definitive motifs of early Brazilian romanticism. Machado, who as a reader and critic had great respect for such Brazilian romantics and Indianists as Gonçalves Dias and José de Alencar,[20] saw in the stories of the New World Indians nativist material that allowed a close examination of universal human behavior and character, problems that increasingly fascinated him. By 1870 Machado, perhaps recognizing his own limitations as a poet, had begun to write less and less poetry and more and more prose fiction. The fact that most of the poems of *Americanas* are lengthy narrative poems may well be, as Ishimatsu suggests, a reflection of Machado's burgeoning interest in narrative.[21]

Not all the thirteen pieces that make up *Americanas* deal specifically with the American Indian, however; eight do, though one, "A Gonçalves Dias" (To Gonçalves Dias), is an elegy. The remaining four deal with such topics from Brazilian history as the Jesuit missionaries, the Inquisition, and slavery. The poems that take up these latter issues also help refute those who believe erroneously that Machado lacked a social conscience. Even here in 1875, three years after his first novel, *Ressurreição,* was published, we see Machado dealing openly with social and political themes of immense importance to Brazil and Brazilians.

With only a few exceptions, such as "Potira," "Niâni," "A cristã nova" (The converted jewess), and "Última jornada" (Final journey), the critics have not failed to pan the tedious didacticism and (for Machado) the surprising stiffness and dryness of these poems. Summing up the majority view on *Americanas,* José Veríssimo believes that in general these poems suffer from, "something rigid, dry, and incommunicative."[22]

One of the poems that at least partially escapes the charge of mediocrity is "Potira," which involves a retelling of the story of an Indian woman who, having converted to Christianity, is captured by Tamoio warriors. This theme, so endemic to North and South American literature that it can be considered a motif, is developed here in unrhymed ten-syllable blank verse. Rather than betray her husband and her new faith by marrying the Tamoio chieftan, Anajê, the woman, Potira, chooses death at her captor's hand. By setting the supposed forces of "civilization" (Potira and all she represents culturally) against those of "barbarism" (represented by Anajê)—and, most importantly, by blurring the distinctions between them—the poem anticipates the psychological analysis of conflicting emotions so powerfully rendered in Machado's later works of fiction. By asking openly, "Que somos nós mais que êles? Raça triste / De Cains, raça eterna" (What are we more than they? A sad race / Of Cains, an eternal race), the poem's voice begins to equate Potira and Anajê in a morally ambiguous amalgam of guilt and innocence, an uncertain universe in which victims and perpetrators continuously change roles.[23]

Without doubt the outstanding single poem of *Americanas*, "Última jornada" is, as Mário de Andrade has perceptively noted, an ironic (and therefore quintessentially Machadoan) reworking of the Paolo and Francesca story in Dante's *Inferno*.[24] A pervasive force in Machado's work, Dante's influence in "Última jornada" essentially parallels the events depicted in canto 5, where the souls of the two ill-starred lovers are swept away by the wind to their eternal resting place. For Paolo and Francesca Machado substitutes an Indian warrior and his bride though, for Machado, only the male figure speaks. But here, as Andrade observes, the similarities end. Whereas for Dante Paolo and Francesca may be considered basically good people, Machado's two main characters are surprisingly portrayed as being largely evil, the woman apparently abandoning her husband, who responds by brutally murdering her. Later, as if by an act of divine retribution, he too, is struck down. Moreover, the souls of Machado's Indians, whose careful characterizations gradually reveal them to be, in prototypically Machadoan fashion, ambiguous mixtures of both good and evil, are never united, as were the souls of Paolo and Francesca. In "Última jornada," with its strong sense of fatalism and resignation, the warrior's soul drifts westward while his bride's soul moves eastward, the two never to become one.

Although *Americanas* differs from both *Crisálidas* and *Falenas* in that it is basically focused on a single theme, and because it consists primarily of long narrative poems, it resembles these earlier works in the mediocrity of its selections (with the notable exception of "Última jornada"). Even *Falenas* is more technically innovative than the very stiffly orthodox, though impeccably correct, blank verse of *Americanas*. In terms of Machado's development as a poet, however, *Americanas* brings to a close what Andrade terms that "phase of cautious mediocrity, in which the genius of Machado de Assis had still not found its true expression."[25] Change was imminent, however, for by 1878, the year he suffered what many believe was a breakdown, Machado had begun to write the vastly superior poems that eventually comprised his final book of poetry, *Ocidentais*.

Published in 1901, *Ocidentais* contains nearly all of Machado's best poetry. Poems like "Círculo vicioso" ("Vicious Circle"), "Uma criatura", (A creature), "A môsca azul" ("The Blue Fly"), "No alto" (On high), "Mundo interior" (Interior world), "Suave mari magno," and "Sonêto de Natal" (Christmas sonnet) are still highly regarded by the critical community as well as the general public. These post-1878 poems, which clearly reflect Machado's definitive break with his earlier romantic tendencies, also parallel thematically the metaphysical and universal issues upon which he expanded so brilliantly in his post-1880 fiction. Although he never gave up poetry writing altogether, after 1880, when he began to realize his potential as a narrativist, Machado wrote only forty to fifty original poems. Some of these, however, such as "The Blue Fly" and "Vicious Circle," and "Mundo interior," number among his finest poetic achievements. Unlike *Crisálidas, Falenas,* and *Americanas, Ocidentais* was not published as a separate volume. Rather, it appeared as one section of *Poesias completas,* a book that was not, as its title suggests, a complete collection of Machado's poetry. *Poesias completas* is a selection of those pieces from the first three published volumes, plus certain poems dating from 1878, that Machado considered his best work. With *Ocidentais,* as Andrade notes, Machado brings Brazilian poetry to the threshold of parnassianism but then abandons it for all practical purposes to create his great narrative works.[26] In terms of Brazilian literary history, then, Machado's *Ocidentais* can be seen as a major precursor of Brazilian parnassianism.

Formally, the poems of *Ocidentais* stand out because of the number of sonnets that appear in it. While he had included only one sonnet ("Luz entre sombras" from *Falenas)* in his first three books of poetry, no fewer than seventeen of the twenty-six original poems in *Ocidentais* are in the sonnet form. Blank verse, which Machado had used so extensively in *Americanas,* is relegated to a minor role in *Ocidentais,* being employed in only three works. Nevertheless, as Ishimatsu makes clear, the ten-syllable line, followed by the French alexandrine, is by far the predominant meter in this collection.[27]

Thematically, the poems of *Ocidentais* fall into two categories: those like "Círculo vicioso," "Uma criatura," "A môsca azul," "No alto," and "Suave mari magno" that express Machado's supposedly "bitter" philosophy or worldview, and those like Spinoza," "Camões," "1802–1885 [Victor Hugo]," "Alencar," and "A Artur de Oliveira, Enfermo," which are tributes to outstanding humanists and friends.[28] Another thematic characteristic of *Ocidentais* is its intense utilization of the dialectical interplay of contrasting forces or sentiments, this being an expanded structural variant of Machado's enthusiasm for antithesis and antithetical pairings. Although Machado had employed this technique in his earlier works, in *Ocidentais* it is dominant. So pervasive is this dialectic between opposites—love versus self-love, good versus evil, or appearance versus reality, for example—that it amounts to a comprehensive statement of the essential weltanschauung of the mature, or post-1880, Machado de Assis. Though this ambivalent attitude about life drives several of the *Ocidentais* poems, nowhere is it more succinctly expressed than in "A môsca azul," a work Goldberg describes as expressing virtually the epitome of Machado's outlook, and "Círculo vicioso," one of Machado's most anthologized poems. Because it sums up so well Machado's

sense of the ambivalence of human existence as well as the conflict between
our attraction to the fanciful illusions of life rather than to its harsh realities,
"The Blue Fly" merits reproduction in full:

It was a blue fly, with wings of gold and carmine,
daughter of China or of Hindustan,
who was born on a certain summer's night
amid the petals of a red, red rose.

And she buzzed and flew, and flew and buzzed,
glittering in the light of the sun
and the moon—brighter than a gem
of the Grand Mogul.

A humble toiler saw her,
and was struck with amazement and sadness.
A humble toiler, asking: "Fly, this glitter that seems rather a dream,
say, who taught it to you?"

Then she, flying around and about, replied:
"I am life, I am the flower of grace,
the paragon of earthly youth,
—I am glory, I am love."

And he stood there, contemplating her,
wrapt like a fakir,
like one utterly dazed
beyond power of comparison or reflection.

Between the wings of the insect, as she flew in space,
appeared something that rose
with all the splendor of a palace,
and he beheld a face that was his own.

It was he,—he was a king,—the king of Cashmire,
who wore upon his bare neck
a huge necklace of opals, and a sapphire
taken from the body of Vishnu.

One hundred radiant women, a hundred exquisite *nayras,*
smilingly display their rare graces
at his feet upon the polished floor,
and all the love they have they give to him.

Mute, gravely on foot, a hundred ugly Ethiopians,
with large ostrich fans,
refresh their perfumed breasts,
voluptuously nude.

Then came glory,—forty conquered kings,
and at last the triumphal tribute
of three hundred nations, and the united felicitations
of western crowns.

But best of all is, that in the open face
of the women and the men,
as in water that shows the clear bottom,
he saw into their hearts.

Then he, extending his callous,
rough hand that was accustomed only to carpentry,
seized the glittering fly,
curious to examine it.

He wished to see it, to discover the cause of the mystery,
and closing his fist around it, smiled
with contentment to think that he held there an empire.
He left for home.

He arrives in excitement, examines
and his mute behavior
is that of a man about to dissect
his illusion.

He dissected it, to such a point, and with such art,
that the fly,
broken, repellent, succumbed; and at this there vanished
that fantastic, subtle vision.

Today, when he passes, anointed with aloes and cardamom,
with an affected air,
they say that he went crazy, and that he doesn't know how he
lost his blue fly.[29]

A model of Machado's parnassian style, "The Blue Fly" combines formal precision and clarity of image with both exoticism and philosophic disillusionment. Written in sixteen four-line strophes, with the first and third lines of each strophe being the longest, the poem possesses (in Portuguese) a rhyme scheme of *a b a b*. Structurally, "The Blue Fly" vacillates between a series of opposites: sensuality versus intellectualism, illusion versus reality, the quotidian versus the exotic, action versus contemplation and comedy, truth versus falsity, among others.

Thematically, however, the poem is dominated by one of Machado's most fundamental concerns—the discrepancy between illusion and reality, between the surface appearance of things and the deeper, eternal truths that lie behind them eluding our best efforts to possess them.

But to this most basic theme Machado introduces a closely related concept, that "dazed beyond power of comparison or reflection," as we humans are by the beautiful though meretricious appearance of life and its entrancing trappings, we seek always to know more about what fascinates us (that is, life itself), to "examine" and "dissect" it. But when we do, we inevitably destroy it, a fact that torments us with frustration and unsated wanting. In having the fly (an insect not ordinarily thought to be beautiful or attractive) say, "I am life, I am the flower of grace, the paragon of earthly youth,—I am glory, I am love," Machado equates life with a fly, thereby creating a wonderfully ironic metaphor to express the absurdity and pathos of the human dilemma. He is suggesting that we struggle mightily to discover true beauty in the dross of reality, but paradoxically when we do discover it and seek to understand it, we destroy precisely what it is that attracts us, and we do so with the same anxious zeal that led us to pursue it in the first place. Ambivalent and inescapably cursed by contradictory impulses, we are our own worst enemies. Life, the "blue fly" that so ardently fascinates us and in which we vainly see ourselves as haughty kings, is the very thing that deceives us and in the end destroys us. There is at work in "The Blue Fly" a resigned or bittersweet irony, a sense that the real truth of human existence lies in its relentless paradoxicality; tormented by our dreams of glory and happiness, we are finally driven mad by our inability to attain them.

Yet as we clearly see in this seminal poem, Machado's world view is not entirely cerebral. Powerfully present here, as in certain other of his works, is a thinly veiled sensuality, a frank realization that to a great degree human identity and motivation are bound up in our concepts of sexuality. Throughout his drama, his poetry, and his fiction, Machado de Assis imbues his characters with a vital though often repressed carnality. For all their intellectualizing, Machado's most memorable characters, from the sophisticated and urbane Sophia of *Philosopher or Dog?* to the "humble toiler" of "The Blue Fly," possess a powerful though muted sexual dimension. Related here to parnassianism's fondness for the exotic, the poem's sensuality is first linked intellectually to the force of life, love, and youth and then in an unabashedly sensual image to a vision of "one hundred radiant women, a hundred exquisite *nayras*" who "smilingly display their rare graces at his feet." This still somewhat restrained image is then immediately expanded into a more overtly erotic one, that of bare female breasts: "Mute, gravely on foot, a hundred ugly Ethiopians, with large ostrich fans, refresh their perfumed breasts, voluptuously nude." Although it is true, as a feminist critic would correctly point out, that several aspects of "The Blue Fly"'s sensuality reflect what could be construed as a "phallocentric" bias stemming from the poem's apparently masculine perspective (the fact that the women display their graces "at his feet," that "all the love they have they give to him," and that they are not only "mute" but "ugly"), it must be remembered that in many other works *(Epitaph of a Small Winner, Philosopher or Dog?,* and *Dom Casmurro,* for example) Machado creates powerful female characters who not only recognize their sensuality but develop it as an integral part of their identity. As "The Blue Fly" makes abundantly clear, Machado de Assis was a writer for whom the sensual dimension of human existence was at least as important as the intellectual, for which he is nevertheless better known. One senses in Machado's work the constant presence of an invigorating human spirit often closely akin to the "jouissance" that Hélène Cixous, Julia Kristeva, Luce Irigaray, and others believe distinguishes much *écriture féminine*. Though typically muted and expressed in symbolic terms, Machado's eroticism is a vital if overlooked part of his art.

Another greatly respected poem from *Ocidentais,* the sonnet "Círculo vicioso" can be taken as a companion piece to "A môsca azul." In Círculo vicioso," however, the central theme focuses more on our eternal dissatisfaction, our insatiable thirst for possessing what we do not possess, for wanting to be something other than what we are. Using a variety of images, both humble and exalted, to move his poem along, Machado suggests that nothing, not even the radiant moon, is content to be what it is: "Dancing in the air, a restless glow-worm wailed, 'Oh, that I might be that radiant star which burns in the eternal blue, like a perpetual candle!' But the star: 'Oh, that I might copy the transparent light that, at the gothic window of a Greek column the beloved, beautiful one sighingly contemplated!' But the moon, gazing at the sun, peevishly: 'Wretched I! Would that I had that vast, undying refulgence with resumes all light in itself!' But the sun, bowing its rutilant crown: 'This brilliant heavenly aureole wearies me. . . . I am burdened by this vast blue canopy. . . . Why was I not born a simple glow-worm?' "[30] By both beginning and ending his poem with a reference to a lowly glowworm, Machado succeeds in generating an atmosphere of ceaseless dissatisfaction, which proves to be ironic in that the majesterial sun, a universal symbol of power and the source of all light, also finally yearns to be something else, to have been born, "a simple glow-worm." Not even the resplendent, life-giving sun, then, itself wearied by its very beauty and brilliance, is immune to dissatisfaction. In having the sun declare, "This brilliant heavenly aureole wearies me. . . . I am burdened by this vast blue canopy. . . ," Machado also injects into this famous poem the sense of *tedium vitae* that, though occasionally discernible in his pre-1880 works, became a trademark of his post-1880 efforts.

"Mundo interior," a less pessimistic poem than either "Uma criatura" or the bleak "Suavi mari magno," conveys Machado's characteristic preference for the complex, interior world of motivation rather than the external world of action and event. A four-stanza sonnet with a rhyme scheme of *a b b a / a b a b / c d c / d e e,* "Mundo interior" (Interior world) sets up a basic dichotomy between the physical world of things and actions and the psychological world of contemplation, motivation, and conjecture. Developing along the lines of the binary oppositions identified in structuralist analysis, "Mundo interior" initially divides into two contrasting but interrelated poems: external nature (described in the first eight lines) and the inner realm (developed in the final six lines). The irony of "seeing" through closed eyes underscores the ontological supremacy of the speaker's inner world, a world acknowledged in the poem's final lines to be both fascinating and compelling but also challenging and disquieting, an "abyss."

The inner world, the tangled realm of consciousness and self-expression, is the speaker's preference even though it lacks the superficial beauty of physical nature. These two worlds are linked, however, in that each is ultimately unknowable in any perfect sense; each possesses "um segrêdo" ("A secret") that simultaneously attracts and repells us. Thus it is that in "Mundo interior," as in so many of his mature works, Machado struggles with the interwoven problems of knowledge, cognitions, truth, and meaning, issues that are at the core of modernist as well as structuralist and poststructuralist theory and aesthetics.

Although Machado wrote relatively few poems after 1880, one composition from this period, the sonnet "A Carolina" (To Caroline) deserves special mention.[31] Written and published (in *Relíquias de casa velha*) in 1906, this moving yet restrained elegy to his beloved wife has established itself as one of Machado's most enduringly popular poems. Patterned on a well-known sonnet by Luís de Camões, "Alma minha gentil," but with a characteristic Machadoan twist, "A Carolina" is charged with the same kind of bittersweet sadness and melancholy that animates Machado's final novel, *Counselor*

Ayres' Memorial, which came out in 1908, two years after "A Carolina."[32] Typifying Machado's unassailable belief in the crucial importance of love in human affairs, "A Carolina" also shows, Blake-like, how the death of a loved one works insidiously to effect the death in life of the survivors, a result the living must not (in contrast to Dom Casmurro) allow to come to pass:

> "To Caroline"
> Beloved, to the marriage bed, the last
> On which you rest from that far life,
> I come, and I shall come, poor dearest,
> To bring you the heart of a companion.
> There beats in it true affection
> Which in spite of all human troubles
> Made our life worth desiring
> And set a whole world in one dark corner.
>   I bring you flowers—remains torn by force
> From the earth which watched us pass together
> And now leaves us dead and apart.
>   And I, if my eyes, mortally wounded,
> Hold thoughts rising out of life
> They are thoughts of what once lived and has ended.[33]

In contrast to Camões's poem, however, in which the speaker hopes to be united with his beloved, the implication of "To Caroline" is that the literal death of Machado's wife has brought about his own figurative "death": I bring you flowers—remains torn by force / From the earth which watched us pass together / And now leaves us dead and apart."[34] The true pain of Machado's loss is evoked in the poem's last stanza, when the speaker, "mortally wounded" yet daring to call to mind thoughts of his companion, thoughts that "rise up out of life," knows all too well that these same thoughts, simultaneously consoling and agonizing, are "of what once lived and has ended."

When *Ocidentais* was published in 1901, Machado de Assis, widely hailed as Brazil's leading man of letters, had been developing his reputation since the late 1870s not through his poetry but through his fiction. Those critics, like Alberto de Oliveira, Ronald de Carvalho, José Maria Belo, and J. Mattoso Câmara Júnior, who have commented on *Ocidentais,* however, agree that in this final collection of poems Machado demonstrates genuine skill as a composer of metaphysically inclined sonnets, the form that predominates in the work.[35] Citing works like "A môsca azul," "Círculo vicioso," "Uma criatura," "O desfecho," "Sonêto de Natal," "A Carolina," "Suave mari

magno," "Mundo interior," and "No alto," the critics have held that
Ocidentais contains Machado's best poetry, the pieces that stand out formally
as well as thematically.

When evaluating Machado de Assis's status as a poet, three issues should
be taken into consideration: first, while perhaps not a great poet, he was at
least in certain instances a very good poet, one who worked diligently to perfect his craft; second, his late poems, those refined and eventually published
in *Ocidentais* as well as those written after its appearance, parallel very closely
the major philosophical themes of his post-1880 fiction; and, third,
Machado, through his omnipresent concern over form and clarity of language, and through his stature as Brazil's foremost writer and critic, must be
credited with having played a major role in the advent of parnassianism in
Brazil. If in sum we cannot classify Machado de Assis as a great poet, we can
certainly say that he was a writer in whom the essence of poetic expression was
a constant and ever vital force.

Chapter Eight
The Plays

Although he only on occasion surpassed the level of mediocrity in it, the theater was very dear to Machado throughout his creative life. Indeed, it was as a playwright that Machado, the aspiring writer, initially wished to make his mark. Beginning in 1857 with *A ópera das janelas* (The opera of the windows) and ending in 1906 (two years before his death) with *Lição de botânica* (A botany lesson), Machado wrote for the theater throughout his career. After 1863, however, the year the critic Quintino Bocaiúva, Machado's friend and colleague on the liberal *Diário do Rio de Janeiro,* pointed out his deficiencies as a dramatist, Machado's activity as a playwright fell off precipitously.[1] The effect of Bocaiúva's perspicacious criticism was such that after 1863, the 1860s being a period of intense theatrical activity in Brazil, "Machado made few attempts actually to stage his plays, being content to see them performed in literary salons with personal friends playing the roles of the characters."[2] Working almost without exception in the genre of comedy, especially romantic comedy, Machado is generally credited with having produced at least thirteen original plays, several operas or comic librettos, a great many theatrical translations (chiefly from French), and a significant body of critical writings concerning the creation of a national theater in Brazil, the nature of drama as a literary genre, and its importance as a tool for raising the political consciousness of the Brazilian people.[3] In terms of these latter issues, Machado's tenure as an official censor for the Conservatório Dramático Brasileiro gave him an important position from which to exercise considerable influence, both theoretically and in terms of what plays were actually presented, toward fostering an authentically Brazilian theater.

As a fledgling playwright and critic, Machado, keenly aware even as a neophyte author, of the close relationship between literature and society, had written that "the theater is for the people what the chorus was for ancient Greek theatre; a moral and civilized initiative . . . without dramatic literature, we cannot aspire to a level of greatness in our civilization."[4] Believing that the artist had a duty to educate and guide his or her society and that the theater was a particularly apt vehicle for the edification of the masses,

Machado strongly favored the one-act comedy, written in both poetry and prose, as the theatrical form most suited to his purposes. Of the thirteen extant plays believed to have been originally written by him, only *Gabriela,* a two-act drama produced in São Paulo in 1862, departs from this general rule. Machado's early theater differs from his early poetry and narrative in that it is almost entirely lacking in the satiric bite, sociopolitical pungency, and universalizing power that distinguish the best of even the pre-1880 works. The early theater of Machado de Assis is on balance that of a callow youth, one possessed of a progressive and idealized view of the artist's role in society but one struggling for critical acceptance. Joel Pontes states it well when he writes that "Machado, the dramatist took no chances. His pieces are part of a general masking of society. . . . His theater adulates society rather than whipping it."[5] Summing up the essentials of Machado's theater by comparing his earlier pieces with his later ones, Pontes concludes that "the final comedies have the same finely educated and respectful of customs characters. There is nothing of adultery, crime, nor the offhand cynicisms or nihilism of Rubião or Braz. The diabolical Machado did not exist for the theater; only the bureaucrat and the bourgeois writer. . . . In this Mário Matos is very correct: '[Machado's] is a theater for the salon, elegant and very polished.' "[6]

Offsetting somewhat this rather cool assessment of Machado's theatrical efforts is the possibility that his efforts in this genre should be interpreted as examples of what has been called dramatic literature rather than as pure theater or drama. When approached from this critical perspective, Machado's plays, which often lack conflict, structural coherence, and movement, seem more aesthetically successful and artistically satisfying than otherwise.

Because many of his plays have been lost, it is not known for certain what Machado's first piece of dramatic literature was. Many critics believe, however, that this honor goes to a comic libretto entitled *A ópera das janelas* (The opera of the windows) that Machado submitted to the Conservatório Dramático when he was eighteen, that is, in 1857.[7] Though it was never produced, the censor's favorable comments concerning its style and originality must certainly have encouraged Machado to pursue his interests in this genre.

In *Hoje avental, amanhã luva* (1860; Today an apron, tomorrow a glove), a work Ishimatsu considers to be Machado's first original book, we have an early one-act comedy in which the influence of French theater is clearly evident, the play itself being an adaptation of Gustave Vattier and Émile de Najac's *Chasse au lion* (1852).[8] The action, of which there is very little, involves two men, Durval, a fortyish gallant, and Bento, a coachman, and two women, Dona Sofia, the apparent object of Durval's amorous intentions, and Rosinha, Sofia's servant and a girl whom Durval had earlier tried to seduce.

The basic plot complication rests on a tangled web of deception, trickery, and lighthearted vengeance initiated by Sofia who in a revealing monologue declares that she will get even with Durval by awakening a sense of jealousy in him. In a surprise conclusion, however, one fully illustrative of Machado's romantic enthusiasm for happy endings, Durval and Rosinha (who in another startling revelation turns out to be less of a servant than a down-on-her-luck equal of Sofia) fall in love with each other, their problems with vengeance and jealousy having been dispensed with. Typical of the formal and thematic weaknesses of many of Machado's plays, *Hoje avental, amanhã luva* is only occasionally redeemed by moments of lively and witty dialogue.

Desencantos (Disenchantments), a two-part "dramatic fantasy," dates from 1861. Apparently never performed, this early play sets up what is basically a comedic debate between two opposing points of view: marriage based on rational and calculated decisions about financial prospects, social status, and material well-being, or marriage based on honest, spontaneous love and mutual attraction between people. This dialectic between differing points of view comes to establish itself as a characteristic of Machado's theater and appears as the essential structural device of a great many other works as well. In *Desencantos,* however, it is the coquettish widow, Clara de Sousa, who argues for a more practical and clear-eyed approach to love and marriage, while the opposite position, that advocating a more romantic and impractical approach, is taken by Luís de Melo, who is dominated for most of the work by the stronger and more forceful Clara, a character who anticipates the later appearing Capitú of the novel *Dom Casmurro.*

Machado's next play, *O caminho da porta* (1862; The way out the door), which, along with its successor, *O protocolo* (1862; Protocol), was published in a volume entitled *Teatro,* shows some technical progress over *Desencantos.* Another one-act comedy featuring three men and a woman, *O caminho da porta* features a somewhat tighter plot, sharper characterizations, and above all a better coordinated and more succinct use of dialogue. The fact that the play's basic plot involves three men wooing the same woman recalls both the early romantic novel, *The Hand and the Glove,* and the story "Aurora sem dia" *(Histórias da meia-noite).* The play ends, once again in a surprising turnaround, when the three men, each in his own way, realizes the futility of what he is doing and heads out in a rush for the door, for the way out (the "caminho da porta"), leaving the formerly coquettish Carlotta unexpectedly alone and anxious.

O protocolo, the *Teatro* companion piece to *O caminho da porta,* is another one-act comedy, this time involving two men and two women. The setting, typical in Machado's theater, is an elegant upper middle-class drawing room.

In many ways, the simple plot of this early play, which turns on a problem of marital discord, presages the more complex conflict in *Dom Casmurro*, where another foursome of men and women become ensnared in a web of love, deceit (real or imagined), and jealousy. In the comedic play, however, unlike the tragic novel, there is a happy outcome. Technically, the play clearly represents progress on Machado's part. Gone, for example, are the constant and heavy-handed literary allusions (typically to classical Greece) that marred the earlier plays. In addition, *O protocolo* shows a marked reduction in its use of conventionally bourgeois love scenes as well as an increased use of a fresher, more natural language.

This development reached its apogee perhaps in Machado's sixth play, *Quase ministro* (1863; Almost a minister), a work that can be regarded as one of his best pieces of theater.[9] Though still suffering from some of the flaws that plagued his other works, *Quase ministro* is the only comedy of Machado de Assis that is genuinely funny. For all its technical and structural faults, it has scenes and lines that make one laugh. Dealing satirically with such universal themes as human greed, hypocrisy, and the fickle winds of political fortune, *Quase ministro* was first represented not on stage but, as was common with Machado, at a literary soirée 23 November 1863 at a Rio de Janeiro amateur theatrical club.[10] The crux of the play, a one-act comedy in prose, concerns a man, Martins, who, we learn at the outset, has reason to think he is about to be named to a high, and therefore influential, ministerial post. This news races through the city and soon is taken as fact. The comic result is that Martins is suddenly besieged by a parade of people who, fawning and fraudulent, are seeking to achieve personal gain or benefit by claiming him as a friend or great solon and beseeching him to grant them favors or sinecures. With each claiming to be more deserving than the others, these office seekers are character types representing a broad spectrum of Rio society. The funniest scene of the play is the penultimate one in which all these idle and self-serving pretenders learn at the same instant that Martins's nomination had only been a speculation, that someone else had been picked. The effect of this news is to send the otiose parasites scrambling for the door in a mad rush to secure an audience with some other governmental minister.

Each of the eight characters in *Quase ministro* is well drawn, and each delivers lines that reveal and amplify his most essential attributes. Other than Martins, the protagonist, and Silveira, his perceptive friend, the play features a series of succinctly depicted character types from Brazilian society: a politically fickle and hypocritical journalist, a vain poetaster, an avaricious inventor (who claims to have invented a cannon that will make Brazil the world's premier military power), an unctuous flatterer who has made a career of ingratiating himself to influential people, a family friend who wants a personal favor, and a foreigner who wants a contract that, in a delightfully ironic parallel with the cannon maker, will permit him to make Brazil the world's premier power in lyrical theater.

In Machado's own meretricious fashion, each of these types argues that the boon he seeks will ultimately be of great benefit to Brazil as a nation. The selfishness, hypocrisy, and greed that lie behind these shallow and pretentious claims suggest that in this play Machado is also satirizing false patriotism, a problem by no means limited to Brazil. By casting both Martins and Silveira as honest and sincere men, and by showing them to be awash in waves of social parasites and frauds (the character types), Machado succeeds here in calling attention to a deplorable dimension of Brazilian society—its corrupt and parochial political system.

The satiric bite of *Quase ministro* is both sharp and artfully restrained, and there is none of the ponderous moralizing that had damaged many of his other dramatic works. The reader, moreover, sees the characters revealing themselves; we witness the characters unwittingly showing their pomposity and fraudulence. The singular vitality of this sixth play derives from Machado's skill at having his characters manifest themselves to the reader rather than rely on the awkward technique of having one character tell the reader what other characters are like. When, for example, the "poet," pretentiously introduces himself by declaring, "Sou filho das musas" ("I am a child of the Muses" [*Obras completas de Machado de Assis*, 28:164]), he unintentionally invites the reader to contrast the hyperbole and ostentation of his words with their paucity of significance. Using the kind of dramatic irony that would later stun readers at the end of *Epitaph of a Small Winner*, Machado here has his six character types reveal the essence of their respective natures by saying things the reader knows to be untrue, grossly exaggerated or deliberately misleading.

The play's structure is tight, logical, and fast paced, with more movement and energy than one finds in most of Machado's dramatic works. In scene 13, where the comic denouement takes place, all the players are assembled together, anxiously awaiting official confirmation of Martins's appointment so that they can press their cases (and disparage those of their competitors). Martins, who has heightened the scene's comedic tension by going out to ascertain whether he was, in fact, named a minister, suddenly returns with the disconcerting news: "Martins: . . . o boato que correu hoje . . . é falso. . . . O ministério está completo, sem mim (". . . the rumor that was going around today . . . is false. . . . The cabinet is complete, without me" [*Obras Completas,* 28:182]).

A collective "Ah!" of recognition and disappointment goes up from the characters, and each one now rushes off in quest of the newly chosen ministers. Extravagantly praised and courted a few moments earlier, Martins, suddenly not in a position to do anything for these people, is now completely ignored by them. The play closes on a note of slightly bitter irony as Silveira recounts an anecdote about a man who, about to be publically executed, is pardoned at the last moment, only to be stoned to death a few minutes later by the mob that had gathered to see him put to death. Pointing to Martins, Silveira asks the favor seekers to be merciful to him, noting metaphorically that he cannot be blamed for either the "conviction" or the "pardon." By thus mirroring Martins's experience with that of the man in Silveira's story, Machado parallels one story in another, thereby deepening the significance of Martins's experience as a reflection of the human condition and not merely an example of the sociopolitical circumstances of a certain Brazilian time and place.

While Martins's story is both underscored and enhanced through its paralleling in Silveira's darkly ironic tale of the condemned man, it is also prefigured in the episode concerning his sorrel horse that he relates at the very beginning of the play. In both anecdotes, the one that opens the play and the one that closes it, an unforeseen event upsets all the carefully laid plans and leads to an unexpected conclusion. In Silveira's first story he is thrown by his horse, while in the second a condemned man is granted a last second pardon only to be murdered minutes later by the crowd of people, now feeling cheated, that had gathered to watch him die. Parallels, both nonironic and ironic, with Martins's experience are thus established at the outset of the play and at its conclusion. They function as metaphors illustrating the capricious nature of human existence that Machado builds into the text of the play in order to advance its basic conflict. These metaphoric parallelisms reflect, then, the fickleness, hypocrisy and violence to which we humans are all too prone. Silveira's two stories prepare the reader for his final, acridly aphoristic line: "Afora os incidentes como o de Botafogo [where he was thrown by his horse]. . . . Um alazão não leva ao poder, mas também não leva à desilusão" ("Besides the incidents like the one at Botafogo. . . . A sorrel won't carry you to power, but neither will it carry you to disillusionment" [*Obras Completas*, 28:184]).

Aside from its physically comic scenes, *Quase ministro* is a fast-moving and tightly orchestrated comedy in which the clear, concise, and natural lines the characters speak are appropriate for the character type each represents. Noting its refreshing lack of a heavy moral and its authentic humor, Pontes describes *Quase Ministro* as Machado's most unjustly forgotten play.[11]

It was, interestingly, the first play Machado wrote after two unexceptional plays, *O caminho da porta* and *O protocolo,* had been damned with faint praise by Machado's friend Quintino Bocaiúva. Noting their lack of dramatic qualities, Bocaiúva had said, "They are attractive because they are well-written. They are valuable, as literary artifacts, but . . . I must tell you that they are cold and without feeling, as are all subjects lacking in soul. . . . Your comedies are to be read and not performed."[12]

Though it is perhaps impossible to judge what effect, if any, Bocaiúva's commentary had on the writing of *Quase ministro,* it is clear that by 1863 Machado had begun to concentrate more on dialogue and character development than on developing the play's social function, which he had advocated a few years before. It also appears that Machado had come to realize his limitations as a dramatist, since after 1863, the year before *Crisálidas* was published, he began to devote more and more time to poetry.

In *As forcas caudinas,* however, a two-act comedy written sometime between 1859 and 1864, Machado was still struggling with drama. This play, which features a story and plot structure similar to those in the short story "Linha reta e linha curva" *(Contos fluminenses),* involves another upper middle-class love intrigue, this time between a recently wedded couple, Seabra and Margarida, and two people who are staying with them as house guests, a young man, Tito, and an attractive but twice widowed young woman, Emília, who is accompanied, curiously enough, by a colonel in the Russian army. The plot is thin to the point of being fatuous: indignant at Tito's seeming indifference to love and, one supposes, to her coquettish charms, Emília, egged on by Margarida, resolves to make Tito fall in love with her. Tito resists, however, explaining that he is disillusioned (one of Machado's basic themes) with love because of having been spurned once before by an ungrateful lover. In act 2, we witness an ironic reversal; Emília, the coquette, ends up falling in love with Tito, whom she had originally wanted only to tease. Tito, however, after making Emília "suffer" unrequited love, suddenly declares his love, explaining that she had been the cause of his earlier disillusionment. In an extraordinary deus ex machina, the colonel then conveniently departs for Russia, having just learned that war has broken out. Since this play could have been written just after the singular *Quase ministro,* one could expect it to be better. As it is, however, the forced and artificial *As forcas caudinas* fails to generate the genuine humor, vitality, and satiric energy of the other comedy. It is not certain, finally, that *As forcas caudinas* was ever performed on stage.

Machado's next theatrical piece, *Os deuses de casaca* (Gods in frock coats), was like *Quase ministro* presented not on stage but at a literary soirée, in this case the 28 December 1865 meeting of the Rio de Janeiro poetry club, the

Arcádia Fluminense.[13] In this one-act comedy, the plot of which involves an "assimilative comparison of human and divine actions,"[14] Machado discusses what might have happened if the Greek gods had decided to live with humans, which they are resolving to do, under Cupid's leadership, at the outset of the play. Jupiter, who resists this idea and scorns humans for their disruptive and violent passions, hypocritical ideas, and vain codes of conduct, can be seen as an early spokesperson for Machado's later, more refined sense of men and women as creatures lost in an indifferent universe and as being destroyed by conflicting passions. Jupiter's tirade against the worth of people conveys a subtle sense of very cautious social criticism, presented more sharply in *Quase ministro*.

There is one particularly successful satirical moment in this play, however. Jupiter, the ruler of the gods, seeks to exert a similar kind of supreme sovereignty over the lives of men and women and therefore chooses to become, as he enters into the human realm, a banker, the perfect symbol of bourgeois and capitalist power during the plutocratic reign of the Second Empire.[15] Jupiter's justification for his transformation into a banker can easily be taken as another sign of Machado's profound understanding of the prevailing social, political, and economic structures of his day. Although, as he suggests in the play's preface, Machado had high hopes for this work, which was written in solid if not spectacular alexandrine verse, it never generated the kind of critical enthusiasm he hoped for.

Also written in verse, Machado's next attempt at theater is the dramatic poem "Uma ode de Anacreonte," first published in *Falenas* (1870). Composed again in alexandrine couplets and involving a love triangle, a virtual motif of Machado's work, "Uma ode de Anacreonte" is, as Ishimatsu notes, both pre-Parnassian in its classical Greek setting and, because it involves betrayals, deceptions, and characters who act out of selfish motives, very Machadoan in theme.[16]

O bote do rapé (The snuff box), published in 1878, is a singularly curious piece. Described as a "seven column comedy" and a "fantasy,"[17] the play, also written in alexandrines, is a cryptic one-act comedy set once again in an upper middle-class Rio de Janeiro drawing room. The plot is extremely simple, to the point of being nonexistent: Tomé, who is ill and unable to go out, wants some snuff. His wife, Elisa, who is making plans to go shopping, offers to get him some. But when she returns, which marks the play's conclusion, we learn that she has forgotten to get it. Her husband, who has in the meantime fallen asleep, dreams about it, however, and this produces the majority of the play's best lines. A strangely fanciful mixture of what seems almost expressionistic theater, a literary satire of Molière's *Dom Juan,* and a comedy of manners,[18] *O*

bote do rapé is Machado's most unusual piece of theater. Featuring a very refined talking nose (Tomé's) that at one point drolly declares, "A nose without
snuff is like a soul without love," this play deserves more recognition for its
experimentalism if nothing else.

Antes da missa (Before Mass), an abbreviated dialogue in verse first published in "O Cruzeiro" (Rio de Janeiro) 7 May 1878 and later produced
under the title "Mexerico à 1880," (Gossip à la 1880), is a transition piece
that shows Machado moving away from didactic theater and toward a more
lyrical one based on aesthetic concepts of art and irony rather than on overt
statements of social or political significance. Written in lively and fresh alexandrines, this brief play is structured entirely around the gossipy banter of
two loquacious Carioca women, Dona Laura and Dona Beatriz, who are on
their way to mass. Their catty barbs are often sharp and revealing of their personalities as well as of their society, which shows clearly how by 1878
Machado had mastered the art of lively and incisive dialogue, the single consistently outstanding feature of his plays.

Machado's continued artistic refinement is evident in the smooth historical play *Tu, só tu, puro amor* (1880; You, only you, pure love). Written as an
occasional piece to commemorate the tricentennial of the death of the Portuguese poet Camões, *Tu, só tu, puro amor* mixes historical fact with creative imagination by focusing on what Camões might have been thinking about his
life and his love for Dona Catarina as he awaited the imposition of his sentence of exile. Since the pain of Camões involves a loss of love—of Catarina
(who may or may not have been a real person), of his friends, and even of his
country—one could argue that this play rests thematically on one of
Machado's fundamental concerns, the consequences that derive from a failure of love. Still by giving the play an allegorical cast Machado lessens this
pain by having it look to the future, to happier days when the force of love
can once again reign supreme in human affairs. Technically, *Tu, só tu, puro
amor* is adroitly done. The basic conflict rests, as is so often the case with
Machado, on a love triangle, here involving Camões and Dona Catarina de
Ataíde (who love each other) and Caminha, a man who loves Catarina but
who, rejected by her, takes vengeance on his rival, Camões, by manipulating
an unjust exile for him. Praised by numerous critics as Machado's outstanding piece of dramatic literature, if not necessarily as theater,[19] *Tu, só tu, puro
amor,* written the same year that *Epitaph of a Small Winner* first appeared, is
the work of a skilled and imaginative writer.

Another outstanding example of Machado's highly refined late theater is
Não consultes médico (Don't consult a doctor), a one-act upper middle-class
comedy dealing yet one more time with the theme of love lost and love re-

gained. Written in 1896, this play's plot complication rests on an ironic though too sudden turnaround. Although marred by some of Machado's old structural problems (awkward transitions between scenes in particular), *Não consultes médico* is largely saved by its lively and genuinely witty dialogue and by scenes that still have the power to make us smile, if not laugh out loud. A good example of Machado's repartee-filled and sophisticated salon comedies, *Não consultes médico* has a happy if disconcertingly abrupt ending when Cavalcante and Carlota, each once spurned in love, conveniently fall in love with each other, thus bearing out albeit ironically the ancient Greek maxim: when "ill" (suffering from love) and seeking a cure (more love), don't consult a doctor; consult someone who has been "ill."

The final play attributable to Machado de Assis is his 1906 one-act comedy, *Lição de botânica* (A botany lesson), a work that provides a technically competent if not brilliant finish for Machado's frustrating career as a playwright. A well constructed, generally fast paced and often funny play, *Lição de botânica* also develops around the structural device of ironic reversal: the play's main character, a Swedish botanist, the baron Segismundo de Kernoberg, plans on giving botany lessons (that is, science lessons) to a young widow, Dona Helena, but it ends up being she who gives lessons (on the need for love in life) to him.

Indeed, the need for love emerges as the play's primary theme. Machado develops the learned baron as a man who has given his life to science, so much so that in his view a life devoted to science has no room in it for love. The play opens, therefore, with the baron asking a widow, Dona Leonor, to close her door to his nephew Henrique, who has fallen in love with Dona Leonor's niece Dona Cecília. Believing that Henrique has a future as a scientist, the baron does not want him to "squander" this potential by getting married. As he explains it to Dona Leonor early in the play, "Henrique is in love with one of your nieces. . . . I ordered him not to come back to your house, but he resisted me. There's only one solution: you will have to close your door to him. . . . Science needs another worker; we cannot enchain him in marriage."[20]

With the "solution" of this initial but secondary conflict presented in terms of a metaphoric act, the shutting of a door, Machado deftly begins to show how the baron has allowed his heart to become like the door he wants Dona Leonor to close to Henrique. So much so, indeed, does the closed door become the play's central metaphor that Machado feels compelled to have Dona Helena, a youthful and attractive widow who ultimately pairs off with a "resurrected" baron, actually give the reader in scene 2 a foreshadowing of the play's conclusion: "There's one thing for sure . . . Il faut qu'une porte soit ouverte ou fermée. The door in this case is the heart" (1172). Although Dona Helena consciously uses the metaphor here to depict the amorous relationship between her niece Dona Cecília and the baron's nephew Henrique, she employs it again in the play's penultimate scene to comment on the nascent relationship between herself and the baron, a man who has just begun to comprehend the revivifying powers of love:

Baron: Dear lady! (He walks to the door and stops). Shall I never again pass through this door?
D. Helena: You've already closed it with your own hands.
Baron: The key is in your hands.

(1185)

Unified by the metaphor of the heart as a door closed to love, *Lição de botânica* is further strengthened by a steady use of witty word play, ironic double entendres, and solid characterizations, especially of Dona Helena and the baron (who recalls Dr. Bacamarte of "The Green House"). Kernoberg, for example, ultimately reveals himself as a prototypically Machodoan character in scene 14, the final scene, when, admitting to the egoism and violence of his past behavior as well as the falsity of his existence, he chooses to undertake a new life, one based not on egoism, violence, and false appearances but on love.[21] At this point the play abruptly ends with the baron asking Dona Leonor that his nephew be permitted to marry Cecília and less expectedly that he, now on the verge of being saved by love, be taken in marriage by Helena. The baron is unique as a Machadoan character, however, because, unlike Felix (of *Ressurreição*), Braz Cubas, or Dom Casmurro, he finally sees how love could rehumanize him, how it could reopen the door of his heart, which he had closed in his obsessive pursuit of scientific knowledge. The play's double-edged final line, delivered by the perceptive and strong willed Dona Helena, that "tudo isto é botânica aplicada" (all this is applied botany), once again demonstrates the mature Machado's singular ability to sum up conflicts in the form of a single, telling, and ironically charged metaphor, one that in this case binds the entire play together by bringing its basic structural process of ironic reversal to a close.

Yet even disregarding a few melodramatic moments, a few awkward scenes and a few moments of forced dialogue and characterization, *Lição de botânica* still suffers from an inconclusive ending. Rather than end the play by having Helena accept the baron's hand in marriage, Machado has Helena demur. Referring to her suitor's "request" for her hand, Dona Helena, showing once again her independence and spunk, coyly declares:

Helena:	It's not enough to ask; you have to achieve.
Baron:	Will I not achieve it?
Helena:	Give me three months of reflection.
Baron:	Three months is an eternity.
Helena:	An eternity of ninety days.
Baron:	After that time, will there be happiness or despair?
Helena:	(Extending him her hand): The choice is in your hands.

(Obra Completa, 2:1186–87; my translation)

Presumably, Machado is suggesting here that the baron will actually have to prove himself during this three-month interregnum, to make his actions match his words. In addition, one feels that Helena will be judging both the baron and her own feelings about the entire affair. This is all well and good; the problem with the play's conclusion has to do with structural unity, however, not theme or characterization. Since Dona Helena has earlier in the play expressed something more than a clinical sympathy for the Baron and his plight, Machado might well have closed the play on a more decisive and less open-ended note. As it is, he admirably reinforces Helena's developing strength and independence as a character, but he does so at considerable cost to the play's unity. One wonders if, through his marvelous powers of characterization, he might have seduced himself into trying to tell too many stories in this final play. While narrative—the genre in which Machado was such an accomplished artist at this point in his career—lends itself to a multiplicity of psychological conflicts, dramatic literature does not.

Although it is far from a perfect play, *Lição de botânica* can also be considered one of Machado's best overall theatrical efforts. More than this, it is without question the one play in which the marvelous technical skills and innovations of Machado, the mature narrativist, are both most evident and most frustrated. In many ways the genres of theater and narrative cannot be reconciled, a point Machado must surely have been acutely aware of in 1906, the year *Lição de botânica* was written.

Although, as Keith Brower, Claude Hulet, Joel Pontes, Mário Matos, Barreto Filho, Sábato Magaldi, and others have suggested,[22] Machado's theatrical efforts almost certainly had a significant influence on the structures and techniques of his later narratives, no extensive study of this important relationship as yet exists. Brower, however, following Hulet, rightly notes that while "the strength of Machado's theater lies in its dialogue," his extensive reliance on it also prevented him from developing any substantial dramatic action and indeed led him both to indulge in oversimplified plots and characters and overly abrupt and illogical endings.[23] One concludes, however, that while Machado's heavy dependence in his plays on an often brilliantly rendered dialogue may have been a detriment to live theater, it was a boon to his novels and stories, narrative being a genre more amenable to the polysemic ironies and ambiguities of language so favored by Machado. While certain of the plays, such as *Quase ministro, Tu, só tu, puro amor,* and *Lição de botânica,* have definite aesthetic value as dramatic literature in and of themselves, there can be but little doubt that on balance one is primarily led to study Machado's plays to see how they fit into the overall artistic growth of a great writer.

Chapter Nine

Literary Theory and Criticism; the Translations; the "Crônicas," Letters and Columns

Criticism and Theory

Machado de Assis always believed that the function of the critic was of paramount importance in the world of letters.[1] While not great in quantity, Machado's literary theory and criticism was astute, perspicacious, and influential. As a critic, moreover, Machado increasingly developed higher levels of sophistication and skill, just as in his theater, poetry, and fiction.

In 1858, at virtually the outset of his career, Machado published one of his most significant critical essays "O passado, o presente e o futuro da literatura" (The past, present, and future of literature), in which, at age nineteen, he argued that Brazil needed an authentic national literature and that for writers society was a mine to be explored, a rich source of characters, types, and problems that should be artistically examined.[2]

A similar position is taken in another of his important early critical statements, "Idéias sôbre o teatro" (1859; Ideas on the theatre), in which he declares, "The theater is not merely a means of conveying propaganda, . . . it is the most effective means, the most reliable, the subtlest. . . . Without dramatic literature, we cannot aspire to great levels of civilization."[3] As indicated in these two fledgling critical statements, Machado initially believed that art, and especially the theater (which, heavily influenced by French theater, was then very much in vogue in Brazil), had a pragmatic function, that it should educate, inspire, and instruct people as well as entertain them.

Though this rather Horatian attitude about the symbiotic relationship between art and life generally characterizes Machado's early phase, his post-1880 work shows him to have developed a very different critical position, one that called for a decisive separation of art and its overtly social or moral function.[4] In the post-1880 works, which both exist on their own as autonomous art objects and yet nevertheless retain a subtle social dimension,

Machado effects a clear distinction between a text's aesthetic and historical truth, the latter being always subservient to the former. In counseling writers (and critics) never to sacrifice this all-important aesthetic truth for historical or "factual" truth, Machado, as Coutinho has observed, was placing himself squarely in the Aristotelian tradition, one in which art is never a mere copy or reproduction of reality but a selective imitation of it, one that transforms and transfigures a particular historical truth into a higher and universal truth.[5]

By calling for an approach to literary criticism in which the critic must first determine what the author intended to do in a particular piece of literature and then judge to what extent he or she attained this goal, Machado de Assis was advocating a critical position very similar to the one being developed at about the same time by James.[6] Like James an admirer of the views of the French critic Charles-Augustin Sainte-Beuve, Machado was essentially a classicist, for whom the classical authors lived not as narrow, rigid, or dogmatic rule givers but as the founders of a living tradition of great and enduring art, which, through its technical and formal control and its thematic universality, has stood the test of time. Seeking this status for his own works, Machado envisioned the republic of letters as being governed by three interconnected bodies: the legislative power (the classical tradition and its "rules"); the executive power (the authors); and the judiciary power (the critics).[7] Machado, again like James, was an extraordinary synthesis of both the creative and the critical spirit. The result is that one can often best appreciate him as a critic when reading him as an imaginative author, as one who practiced what he preached.

Although his basic classicism led him naturally to judge works (including his own) on the strength of how well they compared with the great works of the Western tradition, Machado was far from being a narrow-minded reactionary, however. He was to the contrary a staunch supporter of change and growth in literature, a fact clearly borne out by his praise of several practitioners of the "new," largely antiromantic poetry that was becoming popular in Brazil during the 1870s. His famous essay "A nova geração" (1879; The new generation), for example, is not an undiscriminating blanket endorsement of new trends but a judicious commentary that shows why, when put into practice by talented, imaginative, and discriminating writers (principally poets), these trends would have a salubrious effect on Brazilian literature.[8] In reading this essay as well as others like it, and in recalling the radical innovations displayed in works like *Epitaph of a Small Winner* and *Dom Casmurro,* one can understand that while Machado de Assis may have been "an enemy of improvisation"—a demanding critic for whom a work of literary art was aesthetically valid only if its creation obeyed the rules of literary art[9]—he was also an open-minded artist. Though rejecting improvisation as carelessness and as resulting in bad art, he embraced the vital concept of artistic evolution, aesthetic originality, and innovation and development, the very qualities that characterize his own career as an artist. So, while Machado could not accept change merely for the sake of change, a concept he found frivolous, superficial, and therefore unacceptable, change for the sake of attaining the aesthetic truth that he felt should be the artist's only goal was not only acceptable but perfectly consistent with the classical tradition, which accommodated change that led to superior art.[10] Like Horace Machado believed in studying the classics because it could lead one to discover the principles of the masters, which could become guides for one's own work. To write well for Machado meant avoiding excessive or unnecessary verbiage; it meant restraining one's expression, purifying one's style, seeking always the precise word, and controlling the excitement of the creative act without destroying its sense of spontaneity.[11] Machado took his own critical advice to heart, so much so that by the mid-1890s he was all but unanimously applauded not only as Brazil's leading writer but as its leading critic as well, one whose critical opinion was eagerly sought by the major writers of the day.[12]

If Machado's 1865 essay, "O ideal do crítico" (The ideal of the critic) can be taken as the most succinct and complete statement of what he took the nature and function of criticism to be,[13] his two-part critique of Eça de Queirós's 1878 novel, Cousin Basilio, must surely rank as his single most famous critical statement. A brilliant explication de texte that incisively analyzes the novel's strengths and weaknesses, Machado's study is also a telling indictment of French naturalism, which Machado disdained for being superficial, simplistic, and prone to lurid sensationalism. In certain key respects Machado's objections to Cousin Basilio are similar to those raised by Henry James to Emile Zola's Nana (1880). Both Machado and James criticize the naturalists' thin sense of characterization, their use of ofttimes clumsy plot structures, and their penchant for conflicts that were neither psychological nor ethical in nature. The result, according to Machado (and James), was that naturalistic novels like Cousin Basilio and Nana tended all too often to be dull and worst of all inartistic. Panning the excesses of French naturalism, which he referred to as "realismo," Machado called not for the creation of an analytical and factually precise "reality" but of an artistic reality, one based on the aesthetic principles of selectivity, unity, and logical coherence. Implying that naturalism, because of its basic tenets, was simply incapable of dealing with the manifold complexities (and especially the psychological complexities) of reality, Machado advised writers to scrutinize "reality" but to turn away from the superficiality of naturalism and in so doing avoid having to sacrifice the "verdade estética" (aesthetic truth) that all true art seeks.[14] Fundamentally then Machado's objection to naturalism was that while it might be good sociology, it was bad aesthetics and therefore unacceptable as serious art.

Showing how W. J. Harvey's theory of mimesis and its application to both character and structure in the novel apply to Machado's aesthetic goals, Nunes observes that "all of Machado de Assis's novels are determined by the conflicts of his characters' passions and temperaments. His ultimate esthetic aim for Brazilian literary art was to see the cultivation of the novel uniting the study of human passions to the delicate and original touches of poetry."[15] For Machado this was the only way a writer could avoid the "servile and photographic realism of the school of Zola"[16] and achieve an artistic reality based on aesthetic truth rather than on a rote imitation of three dimensional reality. This point is clearly set forth by Machado in the prefaces to his first two novels, *Ressurreição* and *The Hand and the Glove,* where, already in sharp contrast with the naturalists, he advocates the writing of narratives in which the basic conflict arises from out of the complex and warring natures of the protagonists themselves. Calling him, "a privateer in the service of art," Caldwell sums up Machado's antipathy toward naturalism and the naturalist method: "His criticism of the Naturalist novel was that it aimed at representing superficial appearance—content to be an 'inventory of events and fortuitous' actions unmotivated by human passion and, in its most extreme form, a photographic and slavish reproduction of the low and ignoble—sordid details related for the purpose of politico-social propaganda or with nothing more than a view to arousing momentary physical sensation in the reader, and with no meaning beyond."[17]

Yet, for all that Machado disparaged naturalism, he occasionally found certain of its themes and techniques grist for his own mill. Two of his novels in particular, *Epitaph of a Small Winner* (published two years after his insightful review of Eça's *Cousin Basilio*) and *Philosopher or Dog?,* display numerous elements both of naturalism and its quasi-philosophical analog, positivism, which Machado also held in low regard.[18] While *Epitaph of a Small Winner,* centering on the figure of Braz Cubas, offers a more parodic view of naturalism and positivism, *Philosopher or Dog?,* technically the most conservative of Machado's post-1880 novels, shows him making innovative use of certain naturalist techniques in order to create a powerfully affective but subtle tragedy, one sustained by the presence of psychologically complex and contradictory characters and by a closely interlocking structure of allusion, symbol, and myth. Speaking of Machado's critical awareness of both the advantages and disadvantages of the naturalist method, Nunes writes that "*Philosopher or Dog?* utilizes all the methods of the naturalist novel, multiple angle view of character by the narrator, other characters, and the character himself, accumulation of detail, and free indirect style. . . . *Philosopher or Dog?* . . . illustrates that he was thoroughly at ease in manipulating these techniques which so resemble the processes of the naturalists but he chose not to do so again."[19] So, while as a critic Machado stood in almost total opposition to literary naturalism, as an eclectic and experimental writer he realized that certain of its features could be profitably made use of if one were more interested in psychological probings than in superficial imitations of external realities.

Although, as we see in essays like "O passado, o presente e o futuro da literatura" (1858), "O ideal do crítico" (1865), "O instinto da nacionalidade" (1873; The instinct of nationality), "Eça de Queirós: *O primo basílio*" (1878), and "A nova geração" (1879), Machado wrote literary theory and criticism throughout his career, he began to practice it in a very different way around 1880, the year *Epitaph of a Small Winner* first appeared in installment form in the *Revista Brasileira*. Beginning with this novel, which constitutes a radical departure from his previous work, Machado begins to interpolate his views on literary theory and criticism into the fictional texts themselves. Whereas earlier in his career Machado published critical studies separately, as with his prefaces and the famous pieces on *Cousin Basilio* and the naturalist school, now he submerges his critical and theoretical commentary in the stories he is writing. Appearing in fictional texts and expounded by characters whose reliability in terms of their own veracity is often open to question, these kernels of authentically Machadoan literary criticism are difficult to discern and evaluate, however. The problem is further compounded by Machado's extensive use of parody, irony, and satire. A character may from the reader's perspective be saying absurdities and then suddenly utter a thought that, taken on its own, makes a great deal of sense. Machado also insists, especially in his post-1880 texts, that the reader participate actively in the decoding of these ambiguous and mixed messages. This is precisely what the seemingly insane Quincas Borba does in *Epitaph of a Small Winner* when in chapters 137 and 141 he suddenly advises the apathetic Braz Cubas, "Try to taste life, to enjoy it; and try to understand that the worst philosophy of all is that of the cry-baby who lies down at the edge of the river and bewails the incessant flow of the water. The function of the river is to flow on; adjust yourself to this law of nature and try to take advantage of it" (224). In the context of Quincas's humanitism, an otherwise lunatic parody of Comte's positivism, this singularly positive and rational comment about the need to exercise firm will, courage, and conviction is easily missed. Indeed, this very point is lost on Braz Cubas, who descends ever deeper into the morass of his own crippling egoism, just as it may be on the reader who is not paying close attention. The presence of these authorial statements, embedded within a larger fictional framework, helps explain why, especially in his later works, Machado puts such emphasis on the reader's discriminating participation in the creation of the text's meanings.

Machado also employs this technique in a number of places in *Epitaph of a Small Winner,*[20] notable among which are chapters 55, 71 (in which Braz accuses the reader of being the book's greatest defect), and 138 (in which an exasperated Braz declares to the reader, "Good God, do I have to explain everything!"). Nowhere does he do it so artfully, however, as in chapter 9, "Transition":

Observe now with what skill, with what art, I make the biggest transition in this book. . . . Thus the book has all the advantages of system and method without the rigidity that they generally entail. . . . However, although system is indispensable, one should use it in a spirit of looseness and informality, in one's shirtsleeves and suspenders, like a person who does not care what the lady who lives across the street, or even the policeman on the block, may think of him. It is like eloquence; for there is a genuine and vibrant eloquence, with a natural, engaging art, and a rigid eloquence, starched and empty. (37)

Speaking metafictionally to the reader, Braz is here attempting to justify the unusual structure and style of his narrative. Keeping in mind Machado's exceptional skill at advancing his plot structures by means of symbol, allusion, metaphor, and image rather than by recourse to description or action, one can easily interpret this key passage as a veiled statement of his new *ars poetica*. Although it is perhaps the only instance in which he does so, Braz here is speaking if not necessarily for Machado de Assis then at least in ways that are fully consistent with the post-1880 views on novel writing and narrative structuring held by the author. Moreover, and recalling Machado's classical yet iconoclastic sense that the "rules" of good literature can be broken only to achieve the "aesthetic truth" of serious art, Braz (Machado) here recognizes both the need for a "system," that is, some degree of adherence to literary conventions, and that a writer should "use it" (the "system," or "tradition") to create the "genuine and vibrant eloquence" of new, original art. In other words, Braz's comments can be taken as an accurate reflection of Machado's own post-1880 views on the relationship between the new kind of novel he was advocating (that is, *Epitaph of a Small Winner* itself) and the literary tradition upon which it was so eclectically based. Moreover, if one reads "the lady

who lives across the street" as Machado's puzzled 1880 reader and "the policeman on the block" as the critical establishment of the time, one can easily
envision Machado de Assis casting himself via his fictive alter ego as the imaginative yet tradition-conscious artist who seeks in this novel the "genuine
and vibrant eloquence, with a natural, engaging art" his critically self-
conscious narrator recommends.

Though it is here expressed ironically and metaphorically, and though it
comes from the mouth of an unreliable fictional character, the aesthetic point
argued for by Braz Cubas in chapter 9 incorporates the essential points about
literary tradition and innovation, and about the artist's obligation to seek
"aesthetic truth," that the critic Machado de Assis makes in his "Ideal do
crítico" (1865). If the 1865 critical essay is lucidly written and cogently argued, the 1880 passage, embedded as it is in the metafictional digression of a
very fallible narrator, is perhaps more telling because its very form demonstrates precisely what is being called for in its argument.

Machado de Assis took his role as Brazil's foremost critic as seriously as he
took his position as its leading creative writer. He wrote criticism and literary
theory throughout his career and he considered them to be essential to the
healthy maturation of Brazilian literature. With highly influential theoretical essays like "A nova geração" (1879), which essentially validated the
antiromantic and pre-parnassian movements in Brazil, Machado effectively
changed the course of Brazilian poetry. And in "Eça de Quierós: O primo
basílio" he made manifestly obvious the fundamental artistic weaknesses in
the naturalist novel, which, much to Machado's dismay, was then enjoying
immense popularity in Brazil.[21] Seeking always as a writer and a critic the
representation of eternal aesthetic truth, Machado, whose fundamental classicism could always make allowances for the artistically controlled iconoclasm
of individual genius, firmly established the practice of literary theory and
criticism as invaluable components in the world of Brazilian literature.

Machado as Translator

In addition to his work as a dramatist, poet, fiction writer, and critic,
Machado de Assis was also an active and skilled translator, who produced
twenty-five separate verse translations as well as five "imitations" and para-
graphs in verse.[22] Though after 1870 he published only seven additional
translations, during the preceding fifteen years he rendered at least seventeen
works into Portuguese.[23] Working mostly from French and Spanish texts,
Machado concentrated his efforts during the late 1850s and 1860s primarily
in the genres of drama and poetry. His translations of major prose fiction

works appear to be limited to Hugo's *Travailleurs de la mer* (completed in 1866) and Dickens's *Oliver Twist*, which Machado worked on during the spring and summer of 1870. An early nonfictional essay "A queda que as mulheres têm para os tolos" (The weakness women have for fools) appeared in 1861 and is widely regarded as Machado's first published book. Although he himself described it as a "translation," there is good reason to argue that it was not so much a translation as an imaginative adaptation of Champcenetz's "Petit traité de l'amour des femmes pour les sots."[24]

Machado's translation work in the genre of theater was quite extensive and includes the following pieces: *Pipilet* (1859; a three-act opera adapted from Sue's novel *Les mystères de Paris)*, Octave Feuillet's comedy *Montjoye* (1864), the three-act drama *Suplício de uma mulher* by Émile de Girardin and Dumas fils (1865), *O barbeiro de Sevilha* (1866), a five-act lyrical drama, *O Anjo da meia-noite,* by Théodore Barrière and Edouard Plouvier (1866), Victorien Sardou's comedy *La famille Benoiton* (1867), a work by Alfred de Musset, *Como elas são todas* (1873), and one by Racine, *Os demandistas* (1876). The original versions and dates of two other theatrical translations cannot be determined: *Tributos da mocidade* and *Os burgueses de Paris (Obras completas de Machado de Assis,* vol. 28, "Teatro," Rio de Janeiro: W. M. Jackson, 1955, p. 5).

In the genre of poetry, where his skill as a translator and critic greatly influenced the development of Brazilian literature by exposing it to several invigorating foreign forms and themes, Machado was an even more active translator. A list of his often remarkable poetic translations includes the following works: from *Crisálidas* (1864), "Maria Duplessis" (from "Marie Duplessis" by Dumas fils), "Lúcia" (from "Lucie" by Musset), "A jovem cativa" (from "La jeune captive" by A. Chenier), "Cleopatra" (from *Cleopatra* by Mme de Girardin), "Alpujarra" (from Adam Mickiewicz's *Conrad Wallenrod*), and "As ondinas" (from a poem by Heinrich Heine). While the latter two works, "Alpujarra" and "As ondinas," were based on French translations of the original works, the first four were translated directly from the French. In recreating these typically romantic poems in Portuguese, Machado made a number of changes. In all but "Lúcia" and "Cativa," for example, Machado departed from the original text in some significant way, and in all six poems he altered the meter (usually by shortening the line) and/or the rhyme scheme. In addition, he "either omitted sections of the original or added material of his own (as in 'Maria Duplessis' and 'Alpujarra') or paraphrased rather than translated the original text, as in the case of 'Cleopatra' and 'As Ondinas.'"[25]

Machado's second book of poems, *Falenas* (1869), contained thirteen translations, nine of which apparently pleased Machado enough to be included in his late *Poesias completas*. Three of these translated poems, "Versos a Ema" (from *La dame aux perles* by Dumas fils), "Cegonhas e rodovalhos" (from "Cigognes et turbots" by Louis Bouillet), and "A Elvira" (from a Lamartine poem), had appeared earlier in journals before being included in *Falenas*.[26] The essentially parnassian "Os deuses da Grécia" was translated from a French prose version of the Schiller original and laments the passing of the classical age.[27] Another poem, "A Morte de Ofélia" (The death of Ophelia), is more of a paraphrase than a true translation in that Machado departs rather freely from the structure of the original English version.[28] "O primeiro beijo," a translation of a minor poem by the Chilean author Alberto Blest Gana, dates from 1869 but was not included in *Falenas*. In *Falenas*, the section entitled "Lira chinesa" is composed of eight parnassian and thematically contrastive translations that Machado had made from Judith Walter's *Livre de jade* (1867), "an anthology of Chinese poems which she had translated into French prose."[29] Summing up the significance of "Lira chinesa" to Machado, Jean-Michel Massa, in one of the few critical studies devoted to Machado's work as a translator, has written that this group of eight poems, involving different views of love, was "an exercise de style doublé d'un apprentissage philosophique."[30]

"Cantiga do rosto branco," appearing in *Americanas* (1875), is a translation of a North Americas Indian song that appears in Chateaubriand's "Chanson de la chair blanche," from his *Voyage en Amérique*, while the outstanding "Monólogo de Hamlet" (1873; Hamlet's monologue), done in blank verse, and "Canto 25 do *Inferno*" (1874) appeared in *Ocidentais* under the titles of "To Be or Not to Be" and "Dante" respectively.[31] Also included in *Ocidentais* was Machado's version of Jean de La Fontaine's poem "Os animais iscados da peste" (1886).

Ocidentais (1901), then, contains not only Machado's best original poetry but his best translation work as well. Noting Machado's growth as a translator, Ishimatsu observes that in *Ocidentais* his selection of translations, "included only works by major Western writers . . . in contrast to the selection he had made for his first three volumes."[32]

Arguably Machado's finest translation, his formally creative yet atmospherically faithful version of Poe's "Raven" ("O corvo") admirably demonstrates the "hermeneutic motion" that George Steiner discusses in *After Babel* as his theory of what a perfect translation should seek to do. Undoubtedly attracted by the thematics of Poe's poem, with its emphasis on psychological states rather than on action, its oppressive sense of death and decay, and its presentation of an indifferent and even hostile ambient, Machado performed a radical rewriting of the original poem. By shortening "The Raven"'s long lines, which would have otherwise necessitated some awkwardly lengthy lines in Portuguese, Machado chose to reproduce not the original's form and meter but its dramatic mood, which he achieved to a remarkable degree by recasting the poem in conventional verses of eight, ten, and twelve syllables.[33] The result of this imaginative process of poetic recreation is the following transformation:

> Once upon a midnight dreary, while I pondered
> weak and weary,
> Over many a quaint and curious volume of
> forgotten lore—
> While I nodded, nearly napping, suddenly there
> came a tapping,
> As of someone gently rapping, rapping at my
> chamber door—
> " 'Tis some visitor," I muttered, "tapping at my
> chamber door—
> Only this and nothing more."

> Em certo dia, à hora, à hora
> Da meia-noite que apavora,
> Eu, caindo de sono e exausto de fadiga,
> Ao pé de muita lauda antiga,
> De uma velha doutrina, agora morta,
> Ia pensando, quando ouvi à porta
> Do meu quarto um soar devagarinho,
> E disse estas palavras tais:
> "É alguém que me bate à porta de mansinho;
> "Há de ser isso e nada mais."

Thus, Machado was quite willing to make extensive changes in the form and structure of the original work. So flexible and inventive was he in his approach to translation that one is tempted to say that Machado, ever a cautious and formally conservative craftsman in his own original poetic creations, wrote some of his most fluid, supple, and inventive verses through what was for him the often liberating mechanism of translation. In a sense, then, some of Machado's best poems, like "O corvo," "To Be or Not To Be," and "Dante," are his poetic translations, because they required that otherwise restrictive problems of form or structure had to be handled innovatively in order to preserve a crucial theme, rhythm pattern, tone, or mood.

Machado's creative labor as a literary translator remains one of his most overlooked aspects. As a late nineteenth-century artist and intellectual, he did much through his translations to foster Latin American literature's then nascent cosmopolitanism. As is clear both from the works he chose to translate and from his theoretical writings, Machado was a true literary courier, who realized early that he could play a significant role in the development of a vigorous international connection for New World literature. Of major importance in Brazilian literary history because of the issues of influence and reception that translation involves, as well as the aesthetic issues related to the theory and practice of translation, Machado's numerous translations deserve further study.

The "Crônicas," Letters and Columns

Describing himself as a "carioca enragé," Machado de Assis was an artist and a citizen deeply concerned with all aspects of Brazil's cultural, political and social scene.[34] A voluminous letter writer, an editor or columnist for several different papers and journals[35] and a lifelong "crônista," or chronicle writer, Machado de Assis produced a wealth of nonfiction. His "crônicas" in particular make for fascinating reading, offering insights into Machado the sociopolitical man as well as the artist. Because the "crônicas" served Machado as a kind of laboratory for the technical experimentations that he later employed in his narratives,[36] the relationship between his fiction and his nonfiction is, especially after 1879, an interesting one.

Some of Machado's finest "crônicas" appeared under the heading of "A semana," which was a column on local (Rio de Janeiro), national, and international events and cultural affairs that he wrote for the *Gazeta de Notícias* from 1881 to 1897, while another, "O velho senado" (The old senate), reflects Machado's reportage of and commentary on the debates in the Imperial Senate.[37] Another collection of forty-two "crônicas," called "Ao acaso" (At random) and written between 1864 and 1865 for the *Diário do Rio de Janeiro*, "dealt with a variety of topics but usually covered current literary and theatrical events."[38] Also in 1864 Machado, again showing his interest in both international and national political affairs, contributed under the pseudonym of "Sileno" (one of many pseudonyms he used) a series of ten "crônicas" to the *Revista de Imprensa Acadêmica*. These pieces dealt primarily with the Paraguayan War and the ebb and flow of liberal and conservative fortunes within Brazilian politics. Another important body of "crônicas," "A semana literária," which appeared weekly (from January to July of 1866) in the *Diário do Rio de Janeiro,* afforded Machado an opportunity to comment critically and theoretically on various literary matters. Writing under the pen name of "Manassés," Machado also contributed from 1876 to 1878 a bi-weekly series of "crônicas" on current events for the magazine *Ilustração Brasileira.*

In general, as Gustavo Corção notes, these pieces, which vary greatly in terms of their subject matter, are characterized by an ironic and what Mikhail Bakhtin has termed a "carnavalizing" tendency to deflate the ostensible "importance" of "great events" and to reveal the human and philosophical significance of supposedly "minor" events.[39] Another notable characteristic of Machado's best "crônicas" might be described as his "strategic digressiveness," his skill at making a comment on one issue lead, often in an ironically contrastive fashion, to comments on other, seemingly unrelated topics before returning for closure to the original subject. In his "História de quinze dias," for example *(Ilustração Brasileira,* 15 July 1877), Machado deftly connects a whimsical discussion of the "Cariocas"'s love of Italian opera with a bitter-sweet allusion to the destructive passage of time, while in another column ("A semana," *Gazeta de Notícias,* 22 April 1894) he wryly compares the sub-stantial financial remuneration of singers and chorus girls to the poverty of artists and thinkers like George Sand and Balzac.

Finally, one finds in "O autor de si mesmo" (The author of himself) from "A semana," 16 June 1895, a famous example of how Machado's tragic sense of life and his grimly sardonic outlook could be adapted to the form of the nonfictional "crônica." Linking a depressing Pôrto Alegre news item about a little boy whose parents allowed him to be pecked to death by chickens with an argument about human existence advanced by Schopenhauer in *The World as Will and Representation* (1818), Machado launches into a brilliant if chilling discussion of the roles free will and moral conduct play in human affairs. Metaphorically equating the pathetic story of the fatally abused child and his monstrous parents to the human condition, Machado, working ironi-cally and "deconstructively" through the words and concepts of Schopenhauer himself, "proves" that, contrary to what one might reasonably believe, in "truth" it is really the weak and victimized people of this world who are the guilty ones; Abílio, the text rationally leads us to conclude, not only "deserved" his cruel fate but, according to Schopenhauer's logic, even "caused" it to happen by being unable to prevent it. By setting up in this "crônica" a series of what classical structuralists term binary oppositions, Machado proceeds to show how the essential violence, cruelty, and hypocrisy of human conduct are made painfully manifest in even the most "trivial" of cases.

In other pieces, such as "A reforma pelo jornal" (Reform through journals) 23 October 1859 in *O Espelho,* Machado expresses a liberal proreform political orientation. In still others, such as "Ao redator dos 'Ecos Marítimos' " (To the editor of "Ecos Marítimos") 8 February 1862 in the *Diário de Rio de Janeiro,* his 19 May 1888 piece, published only six days after Brazil's abolition of slavery in the *Gazeta de Notícias,* or his "Canção de piratas" (Pirates' song) 22 July 1894 in the *Gazeta de Notícias,* Machado pungently addresses the exploitation of workers, the consequences deriving from the problematic manner in which abolition was achieved in Brazil, and, using the events at Canudos as his focus, the relativism of sociopolitical "truths," respectively. Three other "crônicas," dating from 23 October 1883, 12 March 1893, and 31 March 1895, all from the *Gazeta de Notícias,* deal with the issues of ideology, meaning, language, and truth that by the 1980s came to be associated with poststructuralism or deconstructive analysis. These latter writings suggest once again that Machado's theories concerning the unstable relationship between language, truth, and reality were far in advance of his time.

Machado's nonfiction, like his translations, constitutes an area of his oeuvre that deserves more attention. Revealing both the politically conscious man and the intellectual artist, these penetrating yet often amusing works show a powerful truth-seeking mind in the process of growth, analysis, and argumentation.

Notes and References

Chapter One

1. Helen Caldwell, *Machado de Assis: The Brazilian Master and His Novels* (Berkeley: University of California Press, 1970), 4. For more information on this issue, see 228–30.

2. Ibid., 4, 220–30.

3. See, for example, his preface to the 1907 edition of *A mão e a luva* or his foreword to *Relíquias de casa velha*. See also his affirmation of these concepts in "A semana," *Gazeta de Notícias* (Rio de Janeiro), 27 December 1896, and "O velho senado," *Revista Brasileira* 14 (June 1898):257–71, and in his letters to Afrânio Peixoto (24 July 1908), and to Carlos Magalhães de Azeredo (2 April 1895 and 26 May 1895), *Obra completa,* vol. 3, "Epistolário." See, also a 1895 article published by Machado's friend and colleague Araripe Júnior, in *Obra crítica de Araipe Junior,* vol. 3 (Rio de Janeiro: Ministério da Educação e Cultura/Casa de Rui Barbosa, 1963), 5–6.

4. See Eloy Pontes, *A vida contradictória de Machado de Assis* (Rio de Janeiro: Editôra José Olympio, 1939), 255; Mário Matos, *Machado de Assis: O homem e a obra* (São Paulo: Companhia Editôra Nacional, 1939), 199–200; and Lúcia Miguel Pereira, *Machado de Assis: Estudo crítico e biográfico,* 5th ed. (Rio de Janeiro: Livraria Olimpio, 1955), 149–50; 156–65; 170; 205–6; 248–49; 272.

5. In a letter from Barth to author, 31 October 1979, he says, "Machado combines the formal firewords of Laurence Sterne's *Tristram Shandy* with the psychological realism of the late 19th Century to produce a . . . bitter, often tender comic fiction which remarkably anticipates 20th century modernist, even post-Modernist writers."

6. Emir Rodríguez Monegal and Thomas Colchie, eds. *The Borzoi Anthology of Latin American Literature,* vol. 1 (New York: Alfred A. Knopf, 1977), 229.

7. L. C. Ishimatsu, *The Poetry of Machado de Assis* (Valencia: Albatros Ediciones Hispanófila, 1984), 43. Other important influences on his work include Chateaubriand Giacomo Leopardi, Heine, and Almeida Garrett.

8. Ibid., 101.

9. Machado, frustrated with an exhausted romanticism, was endlessly fascinated by "reality" but repelled by the superficiality and shallowness of both "realism" and "naturalism." Writing on this important aesthetic point, Coutinho quotes Machado himself as saying, "A realidade é boa, o Realismo é que não presta para nada" (Reality is good; realism is what isn't worth anything, trans., Earl E. Fitz), in *Obra completa,* ed. Afrânio Coutinho et al., 3 vols. (Rio de Janeiro: Editôra José Aguilar, 1962), 1:56.

10. Jack Schmitt and Lorie Ishimatsu, introduction to *The Devil's Church and*

Other Stories (Austin: University of Texas Press, 1977), x.

11. Coutinho, "Estudo crítico," *Obra completa*, 1:43–44. Organizes the influences on Machado's work in the following fashion:

A. Influences in concept, literary technique, and style: 1. Classical Portuguese writers: Camões, Frei Luís de Sousa, Sá de Miranda, Bernardim Ribeiro, João de Barros, Bernardes, Garrett, Filinto Elísio, Camilo 2. Classical Greek and Latin 3. the Bible 4. Shakespeare, Cervantes, Rabelais, Montaigne 5. Merimée, Stendhal, Gautier, Flaubert, Balzac 6. La Rochefoucauld, Diderot, Daudet, de Maupassant, Poe, Xavier de Maistre, Victor Hugo, Lamb, Fielding, Voltaire, Feuillet.

B. Influences in humor: 1. Cervantes and the English writers Swift, Sterne, Dickens, Thackeray.

C. Influences in philosophy, world view, or the human condition: 1. Pascal, Montaigne, Schopenhauer, *Ecclesiastes*, Leopardi.

D. Favorite books: the *Bible, Prometheus, Hamlet, Don Quixote*. To this list one would surely wish to add the name of Dante, whose presence is pervasive in Machado's work.

12. Antônio Cândido, "Esquema de Machado de Assis," *Vários escritos* (São Paulo: Livraria Duas Cidades, 1970).

13. Maria Luisa Nunes, *The Craft of an Absolute Winner* (Westport, Conn.: Greenwood Press, 1983), x.

14. There is some discrepency about exactly what Machado's first published poem was. Roy Cravzow, "Four Collections of Short Stories by Machado de Assis: Romantic Narratives and New Directions" (Ph.d. diss., City University of New York, 1984), cites a sonnet that appeared 3 October 1854 in the Rio de Janeiro paper *O Periódico dos Pobres* (1850–56) as the first work. This position is corroborated by Massaud Moisés in *A história da literatura brasileira*, vol. 2, Romanticismo, Realismo (São Paulo: Editora Cultrix, 1984), 390. Ishimatsu in *Poetry of Machado*, 15–16, also cites a sonnet, "Soneto—A Ilma. Sra. D.P.J.A.," which appeared in *O Periódico dos Pobres* (but on 3 December 1854) as "the first work Machado is known to have published" (16). Caldwell, on the other hand, believes that "Ella" (or "Ela") was "his first published poem" (*Machado de Assis*, 230) and that it appeared 12 January 1855 in the journal *Marmota Fluminense*. This position is supported by the editors of Machado's *Obra completa* (1:70, 91) and by other critics—Massaud Moisés, for example, who also cites "Ela" as Machado's "primeiro escrito" (first writing) and states that it was published in the *Marmota Fluminense* on 12 January 1855, *Literatura Brasileira Através dos Textos*, 8ª edição (São Paulo: Editora Cultrix, 1980), 248.

15. Caldwell, *Machado de Assis*, 16.

16. Helen Caldwell, *The Brazilian Othello of Machado de Assis* (Berkeley: University of California Press, 1960), 1.

17. Caldwell, *Machado de Assis*, 199–211.

Chapter Two

1. See Owen Aldridge, "From Sterne to Machado de Assis," in *The Winged Skull: Bicentenary Conference Papers on Laurence Sterne* (Kent, Ohio: Kent State University Press, 1971), 170–85; See also Nunes, *Craft of a Winner,* 3–17.

2. See Machado's careful praise of such Brazilian romantics as José de Alencar and his *Iracema* and of certain aspects of the poetry of Gonçalves Dias (*Obra completa,* 3:785–901); see also his "crônica" of 25 December 1892.

3. Gibson Walker, "Authors, Speakers, Readers, and Mock Readers," in *Reader Response Criticism,* ed. Jane P. Tompkins (Baltimore: Johns Hopkins University Press, 1980), 1–6, and Gerald Prince, "Introduction to the Study of the Narratee," *Reader Response Criticism,* 7–25; see also Wolfgang Iser, *The Implied Reader* (Baltimore: Johns Hopkins University Press, 1975).

4. Coutinho, "Estudo crítico, trans. E. E. Fitz, 24.

5. Augusto Meyer, *Machado de Assis* (Rio de Janeiro: Livraria São José, 1958).

6. Nunes, *Craft of a Winner,* 5–6.

7. Eugênio Gomes, *As influências inglêsas de Machado de Assis* (Bahia, Brazil: 1939); Clotilde Wilson, "Machado de Assis: Encomiast of Lunacy," *Hispania* 32 (May 1949):198–201; Afrânio Coutinho, *A filosofia de Machado de Assis e outros ensaios* (Rio de Janeiro: Vecchi, 1940).

8. *Epitaph of a Small Winner,* trans. William Grossman (New York: Bard/ Avon, 1978), 17. Further references follow in the text.

9. Samuel Putnam, *Marvelous Journey* (New York: Alfred A. Knopf, 1948) 184; see also Arthur Brakel, "Ambiguity and Enigma in Art: The Case of Henry James and Machado de Assis," *Comparative Literature Studies* 19, no. 4 (Winter 1982):442–49.

10. Putnam, *Marvelous Journey,* 178.

11. See Charles Param, "Machado de Assis and Dostoyevsky," *Hispania* 49, no. 1 (March 1966):81–87; Demetrius Basdekis, "Dualism in *Notes from Underground* and in *Dom Casmurro,*" *Revista de Letras da Faculdade de Filosofia, Ciências e Letras de Assis* 5 (1964):117–214.

12. Some who consider Machado to be at least partially a modernist include Gregory Rabassa, Antônio Cândido, and Maria Luisa Nunes.

13. John Gledson, *The Deceptive Realism of Machado de Assis: A Dissenting Interpretation of "Dom Casmurro"* (Liverpool: Francis Cairns, 1984). See also Astrojildo Pereira, *Machado de Assis* (Rio de Janeiro: Livraria São José, 1959), and Roberto Schwarz, *Ao vencedor as batatas* (São Paulo: Livraria Duas Cidades, 1977).

14. "The Modernist Novel" and "The Introverted Novel, Malcolm Bradbury and James McFarlane," in *Modernism,* ed. Malcolm Bradbury and James McFarlane (Hammondsworth: Penguin Books, 1976), 393 and 394–415, respectively.

15. *Philosopher or Dog?,* trans. Clotilde Wilson (New York: Bard/Avon, 1982), 271. Further references follow in the text.

16. Massaud Moisés, introduction to *Ressurreição e a mão e a luva,* (São Paulo: Editora Cultrix, 1968), 20.

Chapter Three

1. Everett W. Knight, *Literature Considered as Philosophy* (London: Routledge & Kegan Paul, 1957), 220.

2. Coutinho, "Estudo crítico," 52–53. Coutinho's thematic divisions of Machado's work are the following: metaphysical questions of human existence; the nature of time in relation to human consciousness and existence; the nature of Machado's characters (in particular, their otiose existences); social themes.

3. Schmitt and Ishimatsu, introduction to *Devil's Church*, x.

4. Caldwell, *Machado de Assis*, 75, and Eugênio Gomes, *Espelho contra espelho* (São Paulo: Instituto Progresso Editorial, 1949), 67.

5. William L. Grossman and Helen Caldwell, introduction to *The Psychiatrist and Other Stories* (Berkeley: University of California Press, 1973), viii–ix.

6. Ishimatsu, *Poetry of Machado*, 118–24.

7. *Obra completa*, 3:167. Trans. Earl E. Fitz.

8. *Dom Casmurro*, trans. Helen Caldwell (Berkeley: University of California Press, 1971), 5. Further references follow in the text.

9. Ishimatsu, *Poetry of Machado*, 104.

10. "Mariana," primary trans., Lorie Ishimatsu, in *Devil's Church*, 121. Further references follow in the text.

11. Isaac Goldberg, *Brazilian Literature* (New York: Alfred A. Knopf, 1922), 148.

12. "To Artur de Oliveira, Ill Man," trans. Isaac Goldberg, *Brazilian Literature*, 153.

13. Eugênio Gomes, "Schopenhauer e Machado de Assis," *Machado de Assis* (Rio de Janeiro: Livraria São José, 1958), 91–98; see also Gledson, *Deceptive Realism*, 165–66.

14. Caldwell, *Machado de Assis*, 3, 5.

15. Irving Howe, "The Idea of the Modern," *Literary Modernism* (Greenwich, Conn.: Fawcett, 1967), 11–40.

16. Ishimatsu, *Poetry of Machado*, 120.

17. "The Secret Heart," trans. Helen Caldwell, in *Psychiatrist*, 73.

18. Meyer, *Machado de Assis* (Rio de Janeiro: Edição da Organização Simões, 1952), 34, 41, 43, 77–82, passim; Caldwell, *Brazilian Othello*, 111–12.

19. "A semana," 28 February 1897, *Obra completa*, 3:769; see also José Veríssimo, "Machado de Assis: Impressões e reminiscências," *Revista do Livro* 2 (March 1957):156; and Caldwell, *Machado de Assis*, 111–12. Schmitt and Ishimatsu are two more commentators who see in Machado's "staunch aesthetic moralism" a refutation of his alleged pessimism. (introduction to *Devil's Church*, xi).

20. Albert I. Bagby, Jr., introduction to *Iaiá Garcia* (Lexington: University Press of Kentucky, 1977), xix–xx.

Chapter Four

1. Suzanne Langer, *Philosophy in a New Key* (New York: Mentor Books, 1948), 79.

2. Coutinho, "Estudo crítico," 38.

3. Barreto Filho, *Introdução a Machado de Assis* (Rio de Janeiro: Livraria Agir Editôra, 1947), 75; 154, and passim.

4. "Miss Dollar," in *Obra completa,* 2:27. The female image developed in the second paragraph of this story parallels the central image of the poem "Pálida Elvira." Trans., Earl E. Fitz.

5. Coutinho, "Estudo crítico," trans. E. E. Fitz, 51; Roman Jakobson, "Two Aspects of Language and Two Types of Aphasic Disturbances," *Fundamentals of Language,* by Roman Jakobson and Morris Halle (The Hague: Mouton, 1956), 55–82, esp. 76–82.

6. Augusto Meyer, "*Quincas Borba*," *Correio da Manha* (Rio de Janeiro) 28 February 1959, cited by Coutinho, "*Estudo crítico,* 51. Trans., Earl E. Fitz.

7. See Gomes, *Influências inglêsas, Machado de Assis* and "O testamento estético de Machado de Assis," *Obra completa,* 3: 1097–1120; *Literature in Brazil,* trans. Gregory Rabassa, (New York: Columbia University Press, 1969), "Symbolism, Impressionism, Modernism," 176–254; Caldwell, *Machado de Assis;* Nunes, *Craft of a Winner.*

8. Alfred MacAdam, *Modern Latin American Narratives* (Chicago: University of Chicago Press, 1977), 1–28.

9. David Lodge, "The Language of Modernist Fiction: Metaphor and Metonymy," in *Modernism,* 484.

10. Augusto Meyer, "O romance machadiano," *Correio da Manhã* (Rio de Janeiro), 15 February 1959.

11. Earl E. Fitz, "The Influence of Machado de Assis on John Barth's *The Floating Opera,*" *Comparatist* 10 (May 1986):56–66.

12. Dudley Fitts, review of *Dom Casmurro, New Republic,* 1 June 1953, 20.

13. See Caldwell, *Machado de Assis,* 88–93; see also the many references made elsewhere in the text to Voltaire and Pangloss.

14. Nunes, *Craft of a Winner,* 11–16 and passim.

15. For a more detailed comparative study of Nabokov and Machado see Anne Marie Gill, "The Implied Author/Reader Relationship in *Lolita* and *Dom Casmurro*" (M.A. thesis, Pennsylvania State University, 1984). See Robert Alter, *Partial Magic: The Novel as a Self-Conscious Genre* (Berkeley: University of California Press, 1975).

16. João Ribeiro, *Colmeia* (São Paulo: Monteiro Lobato, 1923), 147–52.

17. John Barth, letter to author, 3 April 1984.

Chapter Five

1. Cf. Chap. 1, n. 14.

2. Machado's first published piece of fiction was a comic short story, "Três tesouros perdidos," which appeared 5 January 1858.

3. Though the exact number is not known, it is certain that Machado wrote more than two hundred stories in his lifetime. Many of these have come to light only recently; see, for example, Cravzow, "Four Collections."

4. Caldwell, *Machado de Assis*, 41.

5. Ibid., 43.

6. *Ressurreição*, in *Obra completa*, 1:192. Trans., Earl E. Fitz.

7. Nunes, *Craft of a Winner*, 25.

8. Ibid., 21.

9. Caldwell, *Machado de Assis*, 49; Wilson Martins, *História da inteligência brasileira*, (São Paulo: Editora Cultrix, 1977), 3:523–25; 535–36.

10. Incest as a theme or motif appears, directly or indirectly, in several of Machado's works; see his stories "Frei simão" (1864), "Possível e impossível" (1867), "A menina dos olhos pardos" (1873–74), "Manuscrito de um sacristão" (1884) and "Casa velha" (1885–86). In the short story "Anecdota do cabriolet" (1905), however, Machado wrote of "the real thing," a story of "the elopement of lovers born of the same mother and of a different father and fully aware of their relationship" (Caldwell, *Machado de Assis*, 53).

11. Nunes, *Craft of a Winner*, 35.

12. Caldwell, *Machado de Assis*, 63.

13. *Iaiá Garcia*, 27–28.

14. Nunes, *Craft of a Winner*, 45.

15. Coutinho, "Estudo crítico," 29.

16. Gérard Genette, *Figures III* (Paris: Editions de Seuil, 1972), 267.

17. Sandra Messinger Cypess, "Machado de Assis vs. Brás Cubas: The Narrative Situation of *Memórias Póstumas de Brás Cubas*," *Kentucky Romance Quarterly* 25, no. 3 (1980):355–70.

18. Nunes, *Craft of a Winner*, 54.

19. Caldwell, *Machado de Assis*, 133–34.

20. Ibid., 142.

21. Ibid., 146–48.

22. I borrow the term from Geoffrey Hartman, who uses it in his preface to *Deconstruction and Criticism* (New York: Seabury Press, 1979) to refer to Derrida, Miller, and de Man. Miller, Hartman, and Derrida in particular show an interest in discovering the richness and diversity of a text, which makes their positions as deconstructionists more amenable to texts like *Epitaph of a Small Winner*, "Midnight Mass," and *Dom Casmurro* than de Man's.

23. Monegal, *Borzoi Anthology*, 301.

24. See in particular Derrida *De la grammatologie* (Paris: Editions de Minuit, 1967) and *L'ecriture et la différence* (Paris: Editions du Seuil, 1967), de Man, Allegories of Reading (New Haven: Yale University Press, 1979), Culler, *On Deconstruction* (Ithaca, N.Y.: Cornell University Press, 1982), and Miller "The Critic as Host,"

Deconstruction and Criticism, ed. Harold Bloom et al. (New York: Seabury Press, 1979), 217–53.

25. Derrida distinguishes between "book," which he sees as a "static" construct, and "text," a fluid creative process in which the writer's intentions and the reader's individual interpretation (or for Derrida his or her "deconstruction") of the text merge and remerge in a continuous interaction.

26. Caldwell, without using the terminology of either structuralism or post-structuralism (deconstruction), was among the first critics to perceive that the real drama of *Dom Casmurro* resides not in the moot question of Capitú's alleged infidelity but in Bento's anguished mind.

27. See, for example, Caroline D. Eckhardt, "A Commonsensical Protest against Deconstruction, or, How the Real World at Last Became a Fable," *Thought* 60, no. 238 (September 1985):310–21; Eugene Goodheart, *The Skeptic Disposition in Contemporary Criticism* (Princeton: Princeton University Press, 1984), 9–15, 25–26, 111–35, and Miller, "Critic as Host," 217–53. In the latter piece Miller to a degree like Harold Bloom takes a more "liberal," humanistic view of deconstruction and indeed sees it as an attempt "to resist the totalizing and totalitarian tendencies of criticism" (252).

28. Goodheart, *Skeptic Disposition,* 171.

29. Paul de Man, *Allegories of Reading* (New Haven: Yale University Press, 1979).

30. E. D. Hirsch, Jr., *Validity in Interpretation* (New Haven: Yale University Press, 1967); Gledson, *Deceptive Realism.* Gledson approaches *Dom Casmurro* by following Hirsch's theory of authorial "intention," as outlined in *Validity in Interpretation.*

31. Caldwell, *Machado de Assis,* 165.

32. Nunes, *Craft of a Winner,* 58.

33. Overall, Dante is one of the greatest influences on Machado's work. References and allusions to Dante occur, often in an ironically contrastive way, throughout his poetry, novels, and stories, though they are most prominent in his narratives. See Jean-Michel Massa, "La présence de Dante dans l'oeuvre de Machado de Assis," *Études luso-brésiliennes,* ed. Jean-François Botrel et al. (Paris: Presses Universitaires de France, 1966), 25–32.

34. *Esau and Jacab,* trans. Helen Caldwell (Berkeley: University of California Press, 1966), 11.

35. Nunes, *Craft of a Winner,* 59–62.

36. See the letter (*Obra completa,* vol. 3) from Machado to Alencar, 8 February (p. 1086); also Machado's reply on 19 July 1908 (p. 1090) to a query from José Veríssimo of 18 July 1908. See also Caldwell, *Machado de Assis,* 200, 215–23.

37. Caldwell, *Machado de Assis,* 198–200.

Chapter Six

1. The plot of this early story parallels rather closely the plot of *Dom Casmurro*.
2. See Cravzow, "Four Collections."
3. See Schmitt and Ishimatsu, introduction to *Devil's Church*, ix.
4. Mário Matos, "Machado de Assis: Contador de Histórias," *Obra completa*, 2:11–24.
5. Schmitt and Ishimatsu, introduction to *Devil's Church*, x.
6. "The Psychiatrist," trans. William L. Grossman, in *Psychiatrist*, 35.
7. Gomes, *Influências inglêsas*.
8. Most of the stories cited or discussed here can be found in the following three collections: *Brazilian Tales*, trans. with an introduction by Isaac Goldberg (Boston: International Pocket Library, 1921); *Psychiatrist*, trans. with an introduction by Grossman and Caldwell; and *Devil's Church*, trans. with an introduction by Schmitt and Ishimatsu.
9. Except for "Admiral's Night," which can be found in *Psychiatrist*, all these stories are included in *Devil's Church*.
10. "Alexandrian Tale," primary trans., Ishimatsu, in *Devil's Church*, 22.
11. Schmitt and Ishimatsu, introduction to *Devil's Church*, xii.
12. "Life" and "The Fortune Teller" (plus a different version of "The Companion," done by Goldberg, entitled "The Attendant's Confession") can be found in *Brazilian Tales*.
13. "The Companion," primary trans., Schmitt, in *Devil's Church*, 77. Further references follow in the text.
14. "Midnight Mass," trans. William L. Grossman, *Psychiatrist*, 94. Further references follow in the text.
15. The Portuguese is: "Vá, vá não se faça."
16. "Mariana" is in *Devil's Church*, and "The Animal Game" is in *Psychiatrist*.

Chapter Seven

1. See Chap. 1, n. 14.
2. Ishimatsu, *Poetry of Machado*, 9.
3. Though the list varies according to the critic involved, the following poems have earned general critical acclaim: "A môsca azul," "Círculo vicioso," "Uma criatura," "O desfecho," "Sonêto de Natal," "A Carolina," "Suave mari magno," "Mundo interior," and "No alto."
4. Goldberg, *Brazilian Literature*, 144.
5. There is some reason to believe that in his later years Machado was at least an agnostic if not an atheist. Regardless, however, there is no doubt that Machado believed in an intensely moral and ethical code of conduct.
6. Jean-Michel Massa, *La jeunesse de Machado de Assis* (Rennes, France: Poitiers, 1969), 431. See also Machado's own letter of 2 March 1869 to his fiancée, Carolina (*Obra completa*, 3:1029–30).

7. The "Christie Affair" of 1862–63 began with a destructive drunken brawl by some English sailors, who were subsequently thrown in jail. The British envoy to Brazil demanded the immediate release of the miscreants, arguing that they had been unjustly detained. When this was not done, British military reprisals against Brazilian ships was threatened, which outraged the Brazilian government and populace alike.

8. Ishimatsu, *Poetry of Machado,* 51.

9. Ibid., 68–70.

10. Machado apparently thought rather highly of several of the poems in *Falenas* because he included seventeen of its original poems (and nine of its translations) in his *Poesias completas.*

11. Ishimatsu, *Poetry of Machado,* 74.

12. In a later (1886) story, "O diplomático," Machado changes this image to read "the green-eyed demon" rather than the "green-eyed muse."

13. Victor Orban, "Machado de Assis. Romancier, conteur et poète," in *Machado de Assis et son oeuvre littéraire* (Paris: M. Louis-Michaud, 1909), 104–5.

14. Ishimatsu, *Poetry of Machado,* 92.

15. César Leal, "Machado de Assis—Poeta," *Estudos Universitários: Revista da Universidade Federal de Pernambuco* (January–March 1966):61–78; ibid., 92.

16. Goldberg, *Brazilian Literature,* 147.

17. Ibid., 147.

18. See José Alexandre Barbosa Lima Sobrinho, "Sílvio Romero e a reação anti-romântica," *Jornal do Brasil,* 14 August 1955, 3–4; see also Ishimatsu, *Poetry of Machado,* 95–96.

19. José Maria Belo, *Novos estudos críticos: Machado de Assis, Joaquim Nabuco e outros artigos* (Rio de Janeiro: Revista dos Tribunais, 1917), 32. Trans., Earl E. Fitz.

20. See Machado de Assis, "O instinto da nacionalidade," *Obra completa,* 3:801–9.

21. Ishimatsu, *Poetry of Machado,* 101.

22. José Veríssimo, "O Sr. Machado de Assis, poeta," in *Estudos de literatura brasileira,* 4th (São Paulo; Universidade de São Paulo, 1977), 56.

23. "Potira," *Obra completa,* 3:103.

24. Mário de Andrade, *Aspectos da literatura brasileira,* 6th ed. (São Paulo: Livraria Martins, 1978), 97–102; Ishimatsu, *Poetry of Machado,* 107.

25. Andrade, *Aspectos,* 97.

26. Ibid., 97.

27. Ishimatsu, *Poetry of Machado,* 116.

28. Ibid., 117; Pereira, *Machado de Assis,* 268, sees "Suave mari magno" as an expression of the shame and fear Machado (supposedly) had at the thought of suffering an epileptic seizure in public.

29. "The Blue Fly," trans. Isaac Goldberg, in *Brazilian Literature,* 152–53.

30. "Vicious Circle," trans. Isaac Goldberg, in *Brazilian Literature,* 153.

31. Some of Machado's best-known poems were written after 1880, however:

see, for example, "Mundo interior," "Soneto de Natal," "A Carolina," "A uma senhora que me pediu versos," "Maria," and "A Felício dos Santos," the last three of which deal rather melancholically with the advent of old age, death, friendship, and one's acceptance of these.

32. Helen Caldwell notes that "the sonnet's second quatrain reminds one of Ayres when he heard Carmo's and Aguiar's hearts beating and felt 'those twenty-five years of harmony and solace' reverberate in his own breast" (*Machado de Assis*, 202).

33. "To Caroline," trans. Ann Stanford, in *Machado de Assis*, by Caldwell, 202.

34. Ishimatsu, *Poetry of Machado*, 135.

35. Alberto de Oliveira, "O soneto brasileiro (De Gregório de Matos a Raimundo Correia)," *Revista de Língua Portuguesa* (November 1920) 34; Ronald de Carvalho, "A poesia de Machado de Assis," *O Diário* (Belo Horizonte), 4 June 1939, n. p.; Belo, *Novos estudos críticos*, 38–39; J. Mattoso Câmara Júnior, "Um soneto de Machado de Assis," *Revista do Livro* 2 (March 1958):70–71.

Chapter Eight

1. Quintino Bocaiúva, "Carta ao autor, Machado de Assis," *Obras ilustradas de Machado de Assis,* 7 vols. (São Paulo: Linográfica Editora, 1968), 3:217–18. Bacaiúva considered that Machado's plays were better read than seen.

2. Keith Brower, "The Theatre of Machado de Assis," *Tinta* 1, no. 4 (Summer 1984):23.

3. The lone exception to his comic production appears to be a two-act drama (now lost) entitled *Gabriela* that, according to Caldwell, was produced on 12 September 1862 in São Paulo; see Caldwell, *Machado de Assis,* 18, 38, and 234, chap. 5, n. 3.

There remains considerable mystery as to the exact number of original plays Machado wrote. Some, perhaps many, are thought to have been lost, misplaced, or misfiled. Caldwell, for example, believes Machado wrote at least nineteen plays and opera librettos (*Machado de Assis,* 16). Of the plays written after 1870, however, only five remain. Joel Pontes, whose *Machado de Assis e o teatro* is the only book-length study of Machado's theater to date, cites (not counting the musical pieces or the lost *O pomo de discórdia*) thirteen original plays known to have been written by Machado de Assis. They are: *Hoje avental, amanhã luva* (1860); *Desencantos* (1861); *O caminho da porta* (1862); *O protocolo* (1862); *Quase ministro* (1863); *As forcas caudinas* (written between 1859 and 1865); *Os deuses de casaca* (1865); *Uma ode de Anacreonte* (ca. 1870); *O bote de rapé* (1878); *Antes da missa* (1878); *tu, só tu, puro amor* (1880); *Não consultes médico* (1896); *Lição de botânica* (ca. 1906). Lorie Ishimatsu also mentions a parody of "La Traviata" ("Cenas da vida do Rio de Janeiro") that Machado coauthored in 1873 (*The Poetry of Machado de Assis,* 97).

Machado's musical pieces, mostly operas or comic librettos, include: *A ópera das janelas* (1857; an original comic libretto); *Pipilet* (1859; an adaptation of Sue's *Mystères de Paris*); *As bodas de Joaninha* (1861; an original one-act opera); and *O remorso vivo* (1867; a four act musical tableau done in collaboration with the poet Joaquim Serra and the Portuguese pianist Artur Napoleão).

4. "Idéias sobre o teatro," *Obra completa,* 3:789–98. Unless otherwise indicated, all translations of the essays are by Earl E. Fitz.

5. Joel Pontes, *Machado de Assis e o teatro.* (São Paulo: Ministério de Educação e Cultura, 1960), 17–18; trans., Earl E. Fitz.

6. Ibid., 45.

7. Caldwell, *Machado de Assis,* 37, and Pontes, *Machado e o teatro,* 19. There still exists, however, some discrepancy as to precisely what Machado's first theatrical production was. Renard Pérez, for example, says that it was *Hoje avental, amanhã luva* (*Obra completa,* 1:175).

8. Ishimatsu, *Poetry of Machado,* 46.

9. Pontes, too, cites this play as ranking, along with *Tu, só tu, puro amor* and *Lição de botânica,* among Machado's best plays; see *Machado e o teatro,* 41, 44, and passim.

10. Caldwell, *Machado de Assis,* 20; at this same soirée Machado recited his poem "Epitáfio do México." Machado was a popular, respected, and frequent participant at the many soirées sponsored by the various literary and cultural organizations of the time.

11. Pontes, *Machado e o teatro,* 80.

12. Bocaiúva, in *Obras ilustradas,* 3:217. Trans., Earl E. Fitz.

13. Caldwell, *Machado de Assis,* 20–21.

14. Pontes, *Machado e o teatro,* 63–64.

15. Ibid., 66. Note that when Juno becomes a woman in this play she is called Corina; one wonders if there could be some link here between the Juno/Corina character in *Deuses em casaca* and "Versos a Corina," one of the more memorable poems from *Crisálidas* (1869).

16. Ishimatsu, *Poetry of Machado,* 88.

17. Pontes, *Machado e o teatro,* 36.

18. Ibid., 62.

19. See Pontes, *Machado e o teatro,* 70–76, and Moisés, *História da literatura brasileira,* 396.

20. *Lição de botânica, Obra completa,* 2:1174; Trans., Earl E. Fitz. Further references follow in the text.

21. What the baron says is, "Todo eu sou aparências, minha senhora, aparências de homem, de linguagem e até de ciência." (I am made of entirely of appearances, dear lady, the appearances of a man, of language and even of science). Pontes believes this revelation presages what he takes to be a similar revelation by Rubião in *Philosopher or Dog?* and by Braz Cubas ("Negatives") in *Epitaph of a Small Winner* (*Machado e o teatro,* 82).

22. See, for example, Claude L. Hulet, *Brazilian Literature,* vol. 2, *1880–1920* (Washington, D.C.: Georgetown University Press, 1974), 96–97, and Sábato

Magaldi, *Panorama do teatro brasileiro* (São Paulo: Difusão Européia do Livro, 1962).
23. Keith Brower, "The Theatre of Machado de Assis," *Tinta* 1, no. 4 (1984):2–25.

Chapter Nine

1. See his "O ideal do crítico," *Obra completa,* 3:798–801.
2. "O passado, o presente e o futuro da literatura," *Obra completa,* 3:789.
3. "Idéias sôbre o teatro, 794. Trans., Earl E. Fitz.
4. Coutinho, "Estudo crítico," 56.
5. Ibid., 57.
6. See Henry James, *the Art of the Novel* (New York: Vintage Books, 1956).
7. Tristão de Ataíde, "Machado de Assis, o crítico," *Obra completa,* 3:780.
8. "A nova geração," *Obra completa,* 3:809–36. It is in this famous essay that Machado pans Sílvio Romero's *Cantos de fim do século* for lacking the form and power of true poetry. Romero was so indignant at this negative reception of his poems that he argued in *Machado de Assis, Estudo comparativo de literatura brasileira* (Rio de Janeiro: Laemmert, 1897) for the critical (and creative) superiority of his mentor Tobias Barreto, founder of the Northeastern or Recife School of Criticism, over Machado. Romero remained a lifelong critic of Machado de Assis.
9. Ataíde, "Machado de Assis," trans. E. E. Fitz, 780.
10. This flexible attitude puts Machado in the tradition of such great critics as Aristotle, Longinus, Horace, Dryden, and Johnson.
11. Ataíde, "Machado de Assis," 780.
12. In a 18 February 1868 letter to Machado, the distinguished novelist José de Alencar asks that Machado review Castro Alves' play *Gonzaga.* See Ishimatsu, *Poetry of Machado,* 72–73.
13. In this essay, Machado compares the literary criticism of his day to politics and concludes wryly that both were being practiced by incompetents ("O ideal do crítico," 798).
14. "Eça de Queirós: *O primo basílio,*" *Obra completa,* 3:913; essays originally published 16 and 30 April 1878. For a partial English translation of this essay, see *Eça de Queirós and European Realism,* by Alexander Coleman (New York: New York University Press, 1980), 45–47; 102–3; 124–28; 131.
15. Nunes, *Craft of a Winner,* 10; see also "J. M. de Macedo: *O culto do dever,*" *Obra completa,* 3:843–47.
16. Nunes, *Craft of a Winner,* 15.
17. Caldwell, *Machado de Assis,* 117.
18. Ibid., 113–18; 124–26; 129–34; and Nunes, *Craft of a Winner,* 7, 15, 21, 50, 74, 101, 143, and 171.
19. Nunes, *Craft of a Winner,* 138.
20. See, for example, the following sections of the novel: "To the Reader," and

chaps. 124, 130, 136, 139 and 140, among others. See also *Dom Casmurro*, chaps. 2, 14, 17, 33, 45, 57, 59, 79, 80, 106, 119, and 148.

21. Caldwell notes (*Machado de Assis,* 117–18) that in all of 1881 Machado's *Epitaph of a Small Winner* generated only three reviews while Aluísio Azevedo's vastly inferior naturalist novel, *The Mulatto,* generated more than one hundred. In opposing naturalism, Machado was keenly aware of bucking the critical tide and popular taste of his time.

22. Ishimatsu, *Poetry of Machado,* 9, 128.

23. Caldwell, *Machado de Assis,* 16.

24. Caldwell, too, believes Machado's piece is not a translation, arguing that the two works differ markedly in terms of the presentation of their basic ideas; while Champcenetz concentrates on the supposedly "bad" nature of women, Machado focuses on men, specifically on the difference between "tolos" (fools) and "homens de espírito" (men of spirit) (ibid., 232). Ishimatsu, however, calls *Queda que as mulheres têm para os tolos* a "translation," but of a work, *De l'amour des femmes pour les sots,* that she attributes to Victor Hénaux (*Poetry of Machado,* 45).

25. Ishimatsu, *Poetry of Machado,* 67.

26. See Chap. 7, n. 2.

27. Ishimatsu, *Poetry of Machado,* 93.

28. It is not known whether Machado worked directly from the English text or whether he used a French translation (ibid., 93).

29. Ibid., 93.

30. Jean-Michel Massa, *Machado de Assis traducteur* (Paris: Poitiers, 1970), 94.

31. See Ishimatsu's discussion of these works, *Poetry of Machado,* 103, 107, 116, 128–30.

32. Ibid., 28.

33. Ibid., 129–30.

34. Machado de Assis, letter to José Veríssimo, 16 February 1901 (*Obra completa,* 3:1056); Machado was an outspoken critic of Rio's then deplorable sanitary conditions and their relationship to the epidemics that often swept the city. In his "História de quinze dias" (1 February, 1 April, 15 April 1877), for example, he wrote about yellow fever, burying alive, and the use of unclean water pipes.

35. Some of these are: the *Marmota Fluminense,* the *Correio Mercantil, O Paraíba, O Espelho,* the *Diário do Rio de Janeiro* (of which Machado was a staff member from 1860 to 67), the *Semana Ilustrada* (Rio de Janeiro, 1860–65), the *Ilustração Brasileira* (1876–78) the *Jornal das Famílias* (Rio de Janeiro, 1863–78), and the *Gazeta de Notícias* (1881–1900). Machado was also a regular contributor to such other leading journals and papers as the *Revista Mensal da Sociedade Ensaios Literários* (Rio de Janeiro), *O Futuro* (Rio de Janeiro), the *Revista da Imprensa Acadêmica* (São Paulo), and the *Jornal do Comérico* (Rio de Janeiro).

36. See Valentim A. Facioli, "A crônica," in *Machado de Assis,* ed. A. Bosi, J. C. Garbuglio, M. Curvello, V. Facioli, et al. (São Paulo: Editora Ática, 1982), 86,

and Sônia Brayner, "Metamorfoses machadianas: O laboratório ficcional," in *Machado de Assis,* 426–28.

37. Helen Caldwell notes and translates portions of some of the "crônicas." See *Machado de Assis,* 3–43. Other collections of Machado's "crônicas," such as "Notas semanais," "Balas de estalo," and "Bons dias," can be found in *Obra completa,* vol. 2.

38. Ishimatsu, *Poetry of Machado,* 71.

39. Gustavo Corção, "Machado de Assis cronista," *Obra completa,* 3:325–31.

Selected Bibliography

PRIMARY SOURCES

Novels

Ressurreição. Rio de Janeiro: B. L. Garnier, Livreiro Editor do Instituto, 1872.
A mão e a luva. Rio de Janeiro: Editôres Gomes de Oliveira, 1874.
Helena. Rio de Janeiro: B. L. Garnier, Livreiro-Editor do Instituto Histórico Brasileiro, 1876.
Yayá Garcia. Rio de Janeiro: G. Vianna & Co., 1878.
Memórias póstumas de Brás Cubas. Rio de Janeiro: Tipografia Nacional, 1881.
Quincas Borba. Rio de Janeiro: B. L. Garnier, Livreiro-Editor, 1891.
Dom Casmurro. Rio de Janeiro and Paris: H. Garnier, Livreiro-Editor, 1900 (though the novel's printing was completed in France by December of 1899, copies did not reach Brazil for distribution until early 1900).
Esaú e Jacó. Rio de Janeiro: H. Garnier, Livreiro-Editor, 1904.
Memorial de Ayres. Rio de Janeiro: H. Garnier, Livreiro-Editor, 1908.

Short Story Collections

Contos fluminenses. Rio de Janeiro and Paris: H. Garnier, Livreiro-Editor, 1869.
Histórias da meia-noite. Rio de Janeiro: B. L. Garnier, Livreiro-Editor do Instituto Histórico, 1873.
Papéis avulsos. Rio de Janeiro: Livraria Lombaerts, 1882.
Histórias sem data. Rio de Janeiro: B. L. Garnier, Livreiro-Editor, 1884.
Várias histórias. Rio de Janeiro and São Paulo: Livraria Laemmert, 1896.
Páginas recolhidas. Rio de Janeiro and Paris: H. Garnier, Livreiro-Editor, 1899.
Relíquias de casa velha. Rio de Janeiro and Paris: H. Garnier, Livreiro-Editor, 1906.
Outros contos, in *Obra completa,* vol. 2. Rio de Janeiro: Editôra José Aguilar, 1962.

Volumes of Poetry

Crisálidas. Rio de Janeiro: Livraria B. L. Garnier, 1864.
Falenas. Rio de Janeiro and Paris: B. L. Garnier and E. Belhatte, 1870.
Americanas. Rio de Janeiro: B. L. Garnier, Livreiro-Editor de Instituto Histórico, 1875.
Poesias completas (contains *Ocidentais*). Rio de Janeiro and Paris: H. Garnier, Livreiro-Editor, 1901.

Theater

Hoje avental, amanhã luva. A Marmota, 20, 23, 27 March 1860.

Desencantos. Rio de Janeiro: Paula Brito: 1861.

O caminho da porta. In *Teatro.* Rio de Janeiro: Tipografia do *Diário do Rio de Janeiro,* 1863.

O Protocolo. In *Teatro.* Rio de Janeiro: Tipografia do *Diário do Rio de Janeiro,* 1863.

Quase ministro. Rio de Janeiro: Tipografia do Livro, 1863(?) or 1864(?).

As forcas caudinas (written between 1859 and 1865). In *Contos sem data,* edited by R. Magalhães. Rio de Janeiro: Editôra Civilização Brasileira, 1956.

Os Deuses de Casaca. Rio de Janeiro: Instituto Artístico, 1866.

Uma ode de Anacreonte. In *Falenas.* Rio de Janeiro and Paris: B. L. Garnier and E. Belhatte 1870.

O bote de rapé. O Cruzeiro (Rio de Janeiro) 77, no. 1 (19 March 1878).

Antes da missa. O Cruzeiro (Rio de Janeiro) (7 May 1878).

Tu, só tu, puro amor (originally titled, "Tu só, tu, puro amor"). *Revista Brasileira,* 1 July 1880. Reprint. Rio de Janeiro: Lombaerts & Cia., 1881.

Não consultes médico. 1896. Reprint in *Teatro.* Rio de Janeiro: Garnier, 1910.

Lição de botânica. In *Teatro.* Rio de Janeiro: Garnier, 1906.

ENGLISH TRANSLATIONS

Novels

Counselor Ayres' Memorial. Translated by Helen Caldwell. Berkeley: University of California Press, 1972.

Dom Casmurro. Translated by Helen Caldwell. Berkeley: University of California Press, 1971.

Epitaph of a Small Winner. Translated by William L. Grossman. New York: Noonday Press, 1952 Reprint. New York: Bard/Avon, 1978.

Esau and Jacob. Translated by Helen Caldwell. Berkeley: University of California Press, 1966.

Helena. Translated by Helen Caldwell. Berkeley: University of California Press, 1984.

Iaiá Garcia. Translated by Albert I. Bagby, Jr. Lexington: University Press of Kentucky, 1977.

Philosopher or Dog? Translated by Clotilde Wilson. New York: Noonday Press, 1954. Reprint. New York: Bard/Avon, 1982.

The Hand and the Glove. Translated by Albert I. Bagby, Jr. Lexington: University Press of Kentucky, 1970.

Yayá Garcia. Translated by R. L. Scott-Buccleuch. London: Peter Owen, 1976.

Stories and Story Collections

Brazilian Tales. Edited and translated by Isaac Goldberg. Boston: International Pocket Library, 1921.

The Devil's Church and Other Stories. Translated by Jack Schmitt and Lorie Ishimatsu. Austin: University of Texas Press, 1977.

The Psychiatrist and Other Stories. Translated by William L. Grossman and Helen Caldwell. Berkeley: University of California Press, 1963.

"The Siamese Academies." Translated by Lorie Ishimatsu. *Latin American Literary Review* 14, no. 27 (January-June 1986):35–41.

Poetry

"The Blue Fly." Translated by Isaac Goldberg. In *Brazilian Literature,* by Isaac Goldberg, 151–52. New York: Alfred A. Knopf, 1922.

"To Caroline," Translated by Ann Stanford. In *Machado de Assis: The Brazilian Master and his Novels,* by Helen Caldwell, 202. Berkeley: University of California Press, 1970.

"Vicious Circle." Translated by Isaac Goldberg. In *Brazilian Literature,* by Isaac Goldberg, 153. New York: Alfred A. Knopf, 1922.

"Christmas Sonnet," by José Bettencourt Machado. *Machado of Brazil,* by José Bettencourt Machado, p. 208. New York: Charles Frank Publications, 1962. This volume also contains translations of "The Blue Fly" (pp. 206–208) and "Vicious Circle" (pp. 204–205).

Collected Writings

Obra completa. Edited by Afrânio Coutinho et al. 3 vols. Rio de Janeiro: Editôra José Aguilar, 1962.

Obra completa. Edited by Henrique de Campos et al. Rio de Janeiro: W. M. Jackson, 1955. 31 vols.

SECONDARY SOURCES

Bibliographies

Bagby, Alberto I., Jr. "Fifteen Years of Machado de Assis: A Critical Annotated Bibliography for 1956–1974," *Hispania* 58 (October 1975):648–83.

Sousa, J. Galante de. *Bibliografia de Machado de Assis.* Rio de Janeiro: Instituto Nacional do Livro, 1955.

———. *Fontes para o estudo de Machado de Assis.* Rio de Janeiro: Instituto Nacional do Livro, 1958.

Books

Barreto Filho, José. *Introdução a Machado de Assis*. Rio de Janeiro: Livraria Agir Editoria, 1947. An excellent close reading of Machado's works; one of the first critical studies not to explicate Machado's texts in terms of his life.

Caldwell, Helen. *The Brazilian Othello of Machado de Assis*. Berkeley. University of California Press, 1960. The first book-length study of Machado in English. Focuses on *Dom Casmurro* and the influence *Othello's* plot had on it. An excellent study and highly recommended.

————. *Machado de Assis: The Brazilian Master and His Novels*. Berkeley: University of California Press, 1970. An outstanding introduction to Machado, his life, and his novels. Includes many illuminating notes from his "crônicas" and letters. Some comments on his plays, poems, stories, and criticism. Highly recommended.

Castello, José de. *Realidade e ilusão em Machado de Assis*. São Paulo: Companhia Editôra Nacional, 1969. Attempts to discern what the author believes are the hidden goals of Machado the artist; covers "crônicas," criticism and theory, poetry, and short stories; an *explicacion de textes*.

Chaves, Flávio Loureiro. *O mundo social do Quincas Borba*. Porto Alegre, Brazil: Movimento Instituto Estadual do Livro, 1974. A Marxist approach to Machado's work; focuses on *Quincas Borba* and responds to earlier studies on Machado such as those by Lúcia Miguel Pereira and Antônio Cândido.

Corção, Gustavo. *O desconcêrto do mundo*. Rio de Janeiro: Livraria Agir Editôra, 1965. Focusing on what he calls Machado's "creative rhythm," Corção discusses the author's pessimism, skepticism, and progressive aesthetic growth; compares Machado to Montaigne and Anatole France; examines the "crônicas" as well as the novels.

Coutinho, Afrânio. *A filosofia de Machado de Assis e outros ensaios*. Rio de Janeiro: Editora Vecchi, 1940. Discusses Machado's interest in the philosophy of Pascal, which the author lamentably tries to link to what he believes is a certain "mulatto psychology" in Machado's work; feels Machado hated life and that the thoughts of Brás Cubas are also his.

Gledson, John. *The Deceptive Realism of Machado de Assis: A Dissenting Interpretation of Dom Casmurro*. Liverpool: Francis Cairns, 1984. A thought-provoking study of *Dom Casmurro;* argues that this famous novel is best read as a piece of literary realism and that it gives the reader an accurate view of the society to which the novelist belongs.

————. *Machado de Assis: Ficção e história*. Rio de Janeiro: Paz e Terra, 1986. A provocative collection of essays that argue that Machado's later works are best appreciated when considered in the historical and political context of the time. Argues that "Casa velha" should be considered not as a short story but as a novel, indeed, as one of Machado's most important works. Highly recommended.

Gomes, Eugênio. *As influências inglesas de Machado de Assis.* Bahia, Brazil, 1939. A landmark study of Machado's work. Focuses on the English writers, such as Shakespeare, Sterne, Swift, Fielding, and Dickens, among others, who influenced Machado's works. Also comments perceptively on Machado's use of humor.

―――――. *Machado de Assis.* Rio de Janeiro: Livraria São José, 1958. An excellent collection of essays on various dimensions of Machado's work; discusses such key issues as his style, his perception as a realistic and naturalistic writer, and the relationship between the artist and society.

Ishimatsu, Lorie. *The Poetry of Machado de Assis,* Valencia, Spain: Albatros Ediciones Hispanófila, 1984. An excellent study of Machado's poetry, including his translations; shows his influences; well documented and clearly written; highly recommended.

Machado, José Bettencourt. *Machado of Brazil: The Life and Times of Machado de Assis, Brazil's Greatest Novelist,* New York: Charles Frank, 1962. This anecdotal and too often simplistic biography of Machado touches on all the salient aspects of Machado's life and times; also comments on selected works in all the genres in which Machado worked: poetry, drama (the author calls *Tu, só tu, meu puro amor* Machado's "best play," p. 133, for example), narrative and criticism; many undocumented quotes; unearthed facts in recent years disprove or cast doubt upon many of the assertions made; an interesting if unreliable read.

Magaldi, Sábato. *Panorama do teatro brasileiro.* São Paulo: Difusão Européia do Livro, 1962. In one chapter, "Preparação de um Romancista," Magaldi argues that Machado failed as a playwright because of his "introspective probing," which could not be transformed into the kind of scenic action needed on the stage; also notes Machado's excellence as a theatrical critic.

Magalhães, Raimundo. *Ao redor de Machado de Assis.* Rio de Janeiro: Editora Civilização Brasileira, 1958. Corrects a number of widespread misconceptions about Machado; shows how in his own way he opposed slavery and racial discrimination in Brazil.

―――――. *Machado de Assis, desconhecido,* 3d ed. Rio de Janeiro: Editora Civilização Brasileira, 1957. Focuses on Machado's lesser-known works and reveals his socially aware and politically progressive dimensions: also discusses Machado's views on God and religion; highly recommended.

Massa, Jean-Michel. *A juventude de Machado de Assis, 1839–1870: Ensaio de biografia intelectual.* Translated by Marco Aurélio de Moura Matos. Rio de Janeiro: Civilização Brasileira, 1971. Widely considered to be the definitive intellectual biography on Machado's early years; highly recommended.

―――――. *Machado de Assis traducteur.* Paris: Poitiers: 1970. A book-length study of Machado's work as a translator. Discusses Machado's skill as a translator, the works he chose to translate, and his techniques. Also comments on Machado's importance as a translator in the development of Brazilian literature in the last half of the nineteenth century; compares Machado's translation of Poe's "The Raven" (O corvo") with Baudelaire's French version, "Le corbeau"; excellent.

Matos, Mário. *O homem e a obra.* São Paulo: Companhia Editora Nacional, 1939. An attempt to explain Machado's characters in terms of what the author believes are key characteristics of his personality and life.

Mattoso Câmara, J. *Ensaios machadianos: Língua e estilo.* Rio de Janeiro: Livraria Acadêmica, 1962. A collection of carefully done critical studies focusing on Machado's unique style; basically linguistic analysis.

Maya, Alcides. *Machado de Assis,* 2d ed. Rio de Janeiro: Publicações da Academia Brasileira, 1942. Like Pujol Maya comments on Machado's philosophical orientation. He also discusses his sense and use of humor and his "pessimism." Maya was one of the first critics (of the pre-1940s era) to place Machado in an international perspective. By comparing him to such writers as Schlegel, Hegel, Sterne, Cervantes, Swift, and Carlyle, Maya effectively situates Machado in the ancient and venerable tradition of philosophy and literature.

Meyer, Augusto. *Machado de Assis.* Rio de Janeiro: Livraria São José, 1958. Discusses Machado's works in the conviction that he was a bitter and subversive misanthrope.

Montello, Josué. *O presidente Machado de Assis.* São Paulo: Livraria Martins Editora, 1961. Through reference to letters, diary entries, and other hitherto unknown writings, shows Machado's interest in the fostering of the Brazilian Academy of Letters.

Nunes, María Luisa. *The Craft of an Absolute Winner: Characterization and Narratology in the Novels of Machado de Assis.* Westport, Conn.: Greenwood Press, 1983. An excellent study focusing on Machado's theory of characterization and his utilization of different narrative techniques; places Machado in the context of great world literature; emphasis on the novels; highly recommended.

Oliveira Lima, M. de. *Machado de Assis et Son Oeuvre Littéraire.* Paris: Librairie Garnier Fréres, 1917. One of the earliest major studies of Machado's art to appear after his death in 1908; the text is an amplication of a eulogy delivered earlier at the Sorbonne; stresses what the author believes are the biographical connections between Machado's life and works and discusses his supposed irony and pessimism; focuses especially on the excellence of Machado's short stories.

Pereira, Astrojildo. *Machado de Assis.* Rio de Janeiro: Livraria São José, 1959. An important study that, without falling into the usual pitfalls of biographical criticism, successfully shows how Machado's fiction also dealt with such sociopolitical themes as the Paraguayan War, slavery, abolition, women's rights, the arranged marriage, the evolution of capitalism in Brazil, and the historical foundations of the republic.

Pereira, Lúcia Miguel. *Machado de Assis: Estudo crítico e biográfico,* 5th ed. Rio de Janeiro: José Olympio, 1955. An ofttimes perceptive analysis of Machado's work but occasionally marred by attempts to explain certain features of his art by reference to his physical ailments, his racial heritage, and his physiognomy.

Pontes, Eloy. *A vida contraditória de Machado de Assis*. Rio de Janeiro: Editôra José Olympio, 1939. Also attempts to explain Machado's themes and characters biographically; touches on such sociopolitical issues as slavery in Brazil.

Pontes, Joel. *Machado de Assis e o teatro*. São Paulo: Ministério de Educação e Cultura, 1960. One of the few book-length studies of Machado's theater; includes critical discussions of the plays.

Pujol, Alfredo. *Machado de Assis*, 2d edition. Rio de Janeiro: Livraria José Olympio, 1934. Pujol's work is famous among Machadoanistas for at least three reasons: it effectively established the legend of Machado de Assis (that he overcame abject poverty to achieve great fame and success); it categorized Machado (rightly or wrongly) as a naturalistic writer (yet one who avoided the excesses of the school); and it called attention to Machado's philosophic dimension.

Reidel, Dirce Cortes. *Metáfora, o espelho de Machado de Assis*. Rio de Janeiro: Livraria Francisco Alves Editora, 1974. A very interesting and useful study that, by focusing on Machado's extraordinary use of metaphor, calls attention to a number of thematic and stylistic features of his work; discusses Machado's work in the context much of post–World War II critical theory; also that of Bakhtin and the "carnivalization" of literature.

————. *O tempo no romance machadeano*. Rio de Janeiro: Livraria São José, 1959. One of the first major studies to examine the nature and function of time in Machado's novels; compares Machado's use of time to Proust's; focuses on *Memórias póstumas de Brás Cubas, Dom Casmurro,* and *Memorial de Ayres;* believes time is a leitmotiv in Machado's work; notes Machado's "modernistic" use of time.

Schwarz, Roberto. *Ao vencedor as batatas*. São Paulo: Duas Cidades, 1977. A Marxist approach to Machado's early fiction; utilizes an socioeconomic analysis of political paternalism as demonstrated in Machado's first four novels; contrasts European and Brazilian romanticism and charts Machado's evolution toward realism.

Soares, Maria Nazaré Lins. *Machado de Assis e a análise da expressão*. Rio de Janeiro: Instituto Nacional do Livro, 1968. Another excellent and comprehensive linguistic analysis of Machado's prose style; recommended.

Parts of Books

Booth, Wayne C. *The Rhetoric of Fiction,* 148. Chicago: University of Chicago Press, 1961. Booth quotes from *Epitaph of a Small Winner* and places this work in the context of his discussion of types of narration; does not comment directly on the novel.

Cândido, Antônio. *Vários escritos,* 12–32. São Paulo: Livraria Duas Cidades, 1970. Notes Machado's blend of the archaic and the modern, his sense of irony and ironic contrast, and his deliberate ambiguity. Believes in contrast to Caldwell that in *Dom Casmurro* it is Capitú and not Bento who causes the tragedy; highly recommended.

Coutinho, Afrânio. *Literature in Brazil*. Translated by Gregory Rabassa. New York: Columbia University Press, 1969, 29–30, 166–67, 178–80, 246–47, and passim. Although Coutinho does not offer any in-depth discussions of Machado's work, he does place it in a number of interesting aesthetic contexts. Under the heading, "Symbolism, Impressionism, Modernism," for example, Coutinho says that Machado, ". . . transfigured realism, a realism broadened by symbolism and mythology" (179); he also discusses Machado's extensive use of symbols, images and metaphors, his "moral idealism," his chronicles and his basic principles of criticism and literary theory; scant but very useful.

Dixon, Paul B. *Reversible Readings: Ambiguity in Four Modern Latin American Novels*, 23–59. University: University of Alabama Press, 1985. Dixon discusses the "ambiguity" of *Dom Casmurro* from several perspectives, including structure and point of view, the use of certain key motifs and metaphors, and the universality of its themes. The author also offers a "metaliterary reading" of this famous work, one in which he believes that, "Bento is to Capitu as the reader is to the text" (51).

Foster, David W. *A Critical Survey of Short Fiction*, 1849–53. Englewood Cliffs, N.J.: Salem Press, 1981. An excellent short description of Machado's short fiction. Notes the characteristics of the Machadoan short story and discusses "A Singular Event" in detail. Highly recommended.

Foster, David William, and Foster, Virginia Ramos, comps. and eds. *Modern Latin American Literature: A Library of Literary Criticism*, vol. 2, 1–18. New York: Frederick Ungar, 1975. A compendium of excerpts from major critical studies of Machado's fiction and poetry; highly recommended.

Goldberg, Isaac. *Brazilian Literature*, 142–64. New York: Alfred A. Knopf, 1922. A solid though general discussion of "The Blue Fly," "Vicious Circle," and other poems as well as of the stories "Life" and "The Attendant's Confession," and the novels *Dom Casmurro* and *Epitaph of a Small Winner*. Compares Machado to Renan and Anatole France.

Hulet, Claude L. *Brazilian Literature*, vol. 2, 95–118. Washington, D.C.: Georgetown University Press, 1974. Offers a concise biography of Machado and a brief critical commentary that points out some of Machado's most salient characteristics as a writer; notes some of the relationships between the theater and the novels; features a very good bibliography.

Leal, César. *Os cavaleiros de Júpiter*. Recife, Brazil: Universidade Federal de Pernambuco, 1969, "A crítica literária no Brasil," 205–16. A brief but perceptive summary of Machado's theoretical and critical principles and an assessment of Machado's place in the history of Brazilian literary theory and criticism.

MacAdam, Alfred. *Modern Latin American Narratives*, 1–28. Chicago: University of Chicago Press, 1977. Argues that, typical of Latin American extended narrative, Machado's novels are not really novels at all but satires; focuses on *Dom Casmurro* and *Epitaph of a Small Winner;* higly recommended.

Moisés, Massaud. *História da Literatura Brasileira,* vol. 2, 391–417. São Paulo: Editora Cultrix, 1984. A good critical overview of Machado's novels, stories, poetry, criticism, and "crônicas"; brief but discerning.

Monegal, Emir Rodríguez, and Colchie, Thomas, eds. *The Borzoi Anthology of Latin American Literature,* vol. 1, 299–309. New York: Alfred A. Knopf, 1977. Places Machado in the context of both Brazilian and Latin American narrative; brief commentary on *Dom Casmurro.*

Putnam, Samuel. *Marvelous Journey: A Survey of Four Centuries of Brazilian Writing,* 176–92. New York: Alfred A. Knopf, 1948. A concise overview of Machado's life and work; places Machado in the context of both Brazilian literature and world literature; compares him to Henry James.

Rabassa, Gregory. *O negro na ficção brasileira (1888–1950).* Translated by Ana Maria Martins. Rio de Janeiro: Edições Tempo Brasileiro, 1965. Deals with the treatment of blacks in Brazilian literature; focuses especially on José Lins do Rêgo, Jorge Amado, and Lima Barreto; also discusses people (like Machado de Assis) of mixed racial heritage.

Sayers, Raymond. *The Negro in Brazilian Literature.* New York: Hispanic Institute in the United States, 1956. Deals with works written both about and by blacks in Brazil to the time of emancipation in 1888; chapter 9 focuses on the Negro in the novels of Machado de Assis and the naturalists.

————. *Onze estudos de literatura brasileira.* Translated by Roberto Raposo, 123–76. Rio de Janeiro: Editôra Civilização Brasileira, 1983. Features three excellent essays: Machado's reputation in nineteenth-century Portugal, Machado's "Brazilian Othelo" (which offers a discussion of Caldwell's book on this subject and of *Dom Casmurro*), and music in Machado's work.

Veríssimo, Erico. *Brazilian Literature: An Outline,* 65–77. New York: Macmillan Co., 1945. Contains some interesting if brief comments on Machado and his work by a noted Brazilian writer and critic; assesses his importance as a Brazilian writer.

Articles

Bagby, Alberto J., Jr. "Machado de Assis and Foreign Languages." *Luso-Brazilian Review* 12, no. 2 (Winter 1975):225–33. Discusses Machado in terms of the foreign languages he knew (some of which, as we see in his French and English translation work, he knew very well indeed) and the influences that could therefore have come to him through texts written in the original language.

Barrow, Leo L. "Ingratitude in the Works of Machado de Assis." *Hispania* 49, no. 2 (May 1966):211–17. Traces this important theme through several of Machado's works; discusses its relation to Machado's characters and their outlooks: see "gratitude" always losing out to "ingratitude"; connects Machado's life with his works.

Basdekis, Demetrius. "Dualism in *Notes from Underground* and in *Dom Casmurro.*" *Revista de Letras da Faculdade de Filosofia, Ciências e Letras de Assis,* 5 (1964):117–214. A good close textual comparison of certain passages of these two works; author suggests the Russian could have been a source for Machado.

Brakel, Arthur. "Ambiguity and Enigma in Art: The Case of Henry James and Machado de Assis." *Comparative Literature Studies,* 19, no. 4 (Winter 1982):442–49. By examining *The Sacred Fount, The Aspern Papers, Dom Casmurro,* "Midnight Mass," and "The Liar," the author shows how both Machado and James deliberately create texts that are ambiguous, enigmatic, and open-ended.

Brower, Keith. "The Theater of Machado de Assis." *Tinta* 1, no. 4 (Summer 1984): 21–24. A discussion of Machado's plays, their strengths and weaknesses, and their relation to Machado's fiction.

Callan, Richard J. "Notes on Braz Cubas," *Hispania* 47 (September 1964):530–33. Machado's supposed "pessimism" is debated; Callan argues that at least in the case of *Epitaph of a Small Winner,* Machado wrote "a pessimistic novel with an idealistic, and therefore hopeful purpose."

Carson, Tom. "He Did It His Way: Machado de Assis, Modernist without Portfolio." *Village Voice Literary Supplement,* June 1984, 22–24. Argues that Machado's post-1880 work ranks him as an early modernist (in the European tradition) and as a precursor of European modernism.

Coutinho, Afrânio. "O método de Machado de Assis." *Cadernos Brasileiros* 2, no. 1 (January–March 1960):20–28. A good discussion of Machado's basic techniques; especially useful for its comments on Machado's style.

————. "A crítica literária de Machado de Assis." *Proceedings: Pacific Northwest Conference on Foreign Languages* 23 (1972):55–60. An excellent overview of this greatly overlooked dimension of Machado's work (his criticism).

Cypess, Sandra Messinger. "Machado de Assis vs. Brás Cubas: The Narrative Situation of *Memórias póstumas de Brás Cubas.*" *Kentucky Romance Quarterly* 25 no. 3, (1980):355–70. Focusing on *Memórias póstumas de Brás Cubas,* Cypess argues that the opinions and views expressed by Brás Cubas in his narrative do not reflect those of Machado de Assis.

Decker, Donald M. "Machado de Assis: Short Story Craftsman." *Hispania* 48 (March 1965):76–81. Focuses on Machado's short stories; comments on his style, his tendency (in the stories) toward "equanimity," and his use of irony, satire, and humor; stresses themes and characters.

Dufy, Mary Terese. "Symbolism in *Esaú e Jacó* with Emphasis on Biblical Implication." *Revista de Letras da Faculdade de Filosofia, Ciências e Letras de Assis* 5 (1964):98–116. Focuses on Machado's use of symbols in one of his often overlooked major works; shows their modernity.

Eustis, Christopher. "Time and Narrative Structure in *Memórias póstumas de Brás*

Cubas." *Luso-Brazilian Review* 16, no. 1 (Summer 1979):18–28. A useful study of these two crucial features of this landmark work.

Fitz, Earl E. "The Influence of Machado de Assis on John Barth's *The Floating Opera.*" *Comparatist* 10 (May 1986):56–66. Shows the acknowledged influence *Epitaph of a Small Winner, Dom Casmurro,* and *Philosopher or Dog?* had on the plot structure, style, and characters of Barth's *Floating Opera.*

————. "The First Inter-American Novels: Some Choices and Some Comments." *Comparative Literature Studies* 22, no. 3 (Fall 1985):361–76. Focusing primarily on *Epitaph of a Small Winner,* the author argues that Machado de Assis may well be considered the first truly outstanding novelist of the Americas, antedating by a few years the best work of Henry James.

Gill, Anne-Marie. "*Dom Casmurro* and *Lolita:* Machado among the Metafictionists." *Luso-Brazilian Review* 24, no. 1 (Summer 1987):17–26. In an interesting comparative study, the author argues that both Machado and Nabokov share a "similar postmodernist attitude toward writing and reality." Gill also shows how these two texts merge the modes of mimetic realism with those of self-reflective metafiction. Highly recommended.

Gledson, John. "*Casa Velha:* A Contribution to a Better Understanding of Machado de Assis." *Bulletin of Hispanic Studies* 60 (1983):31–48. A good study of what the author believes is one of Machado's great but overlooked works.

Gomes, Eugênio. "Quincas Borba." *Cadernos Brasileiros* 2, no. 2 (1960):24–32. Written by a critic often called "the dean" of Machado scholars, this short but incisive piece provides a good overview of one of Machado's most underestimated major novels.

————. "Introdução às crônicas de Machado de Assis." *Cadernos Brasileiros* (Rio de Janeiro) 5, 2 (1963):15–20. An excellent overview of Machado's chronicles, their diverse styles, their themes, and the circumstances under which they were written (periods of great turmoil, nationally and internationally, for Brazil, such as the Paraguayan War, 1864–70; the emancipation of the slaves, 1888; and the founding of the Republic, 1889).

Grossman, William L. "The Irony of Machado de Assis." *Commonweal,* 26 February 1954, 517–20. The author assumes that the "pessimistic" opinions of Braz Cubas are those of Machado himself. One of Machado's English language translators, Grossman here discusses Machado's philosophical outlook (and those of his major characters) in terms of his response to Comte and Pascal; also discusses Machado in the philosophic tradition that later included Darwin and Nietzsche.

————. "A Stifled Yearning for Grace." *Saturday Review* 43 (19 March 1960):20. In reviewing Cecil Hemley's *The Experience,* Grossman points out Hemley's debt to Machado, a debt Hemley openly acknowledges.

Hughes, John B. "El princípio-Brás Cubas: Contemporaneidad." *Nueva Narrativa Hispanoamericanas* 3, no. 1 (January 1973):25–30. Terms *As memórias póstumas de Brás Cubas* Latin America's first "nueva novela" (new novel); using some of the terminology of structuralist analysis, argues that it reads as if it were a contemporary novel; calls Brás Cubas Machado's "Doppelgänger" and believes that Machado's "doubles" are comparable to those created by such writers as Dostoievsky, Guimarães Rosa, and Julio Cortázar.

Leal, César. "Machado de Assis—Poeta." *Estudos Universitários: Revista da Universidade Federal de Pernambuco* (January–March 1966):61–78. Reprinted in *Os cavaleiros de Júpiter.* Recife, Brazil: Universidade Federal de Pernambuco, 1969, 107–26. A good evaluation of Machado's poetry; discusses both Machado's skills and weaknesses as a poet; sees the influence of Gógora in "Pálida Elvira"; praises "Quando ela fala" as one of Machado's better poems.

MacAdam, Alfred J. "Rereading *Ressurreição.*" *Luso-Brazilian Review* 9, no. 2 (Winter 1972):47–57. Argues that *Ressurreição* is neither a "novel" nor a "romance" but a "satire" and one of Machado's major efforts, a "decisive step" in his evaluation as an important narrativist of the postromantic era. Highly recommended.

MacNicoll, Murray Graeme. "Machado de Assis in 1878." *Luso-Brazilian Review* 19, no. 1 (Summer 1982):31–38. Discusses the year 1878 as a crucial turning point in Machado's career; believes *Epitaph of a Small Winner* antedates the work of such writers as Proust, Joyce, and Kafka.

Massa, Jean-Michel. "La bibliothèque de Machado de Assis." *Revista do Livro* 6, nos. 21–22 (March–June 1961):195–238. An excellent summary of Machado's personal library; shows how widely read Machado was and how his tastes ran from philosophy to politics and from history to literature; shows the influence of Poe and Longfellow on Machado (who was interested in the literature of the United States); highly recommended.

Mayersberg, Paul. "A Brazilian Writer." *Listener,* 28 January 1965, 155–56. Places Machado in both a Latin American and a universal literary tradition; argues that Machado is a true literary precursor of Borges; discusses "The Looking Glass" by comparing it to de Maupassant's "Cemetary Walkers."

Moisés, Massaud. "Machado de Assis e o realismo." *Anhembia,* 35, no. 105 (August 1959):469–79. Written by another major Brazilian critic, this short study discusses Machado as a realist and in terms of his relationship to naturalism (which Machado referred to as "realismo").

Newman, Penny. "'O lustre do meu nome': uma Leitura de *A Mão e a Luva.*" *The Luso-Brazilian Review* 20, no. 2 (Winter 1983):232–40. Focuses on the female character of Guiomar in *The Hand of the Glove* and argues that Machado's treatment of women characters has important sociological and political implications; asserts that (in this overlooked early novel's surprising conclusion—surprising in that Guiomar seems suddenly so passive) Guiomar is not nearly as free and as self-determining as she appears; and suggests that Machado was keenly aware of how discriminated against women were in his time and place and that he subtly shows this in the captivating figure of Guiomar. Highly recommended.

Nist, John. "The Short Stories of Machado de Assis." *Arizona Quarterly* 24 (Spring 1968):5–22. Discusses Machado's philosophic orientation, his commitment to the search for universal truths, and his brilliance as a short story writer; says he may be the supreme American prose writer of his time.

Nunes, Maria Luisa. "Machado de Assis's Theory of the Novel." *Latin American Literary Review* 4, no. 7 (Fall–Winter 1975):57–66. A good survey of the various techniques, some avant-garde, some traditional, that Machado utilized; stresses the autonomy of his texts, his call for active reader participation, and his experiments with time, characterization, and point of view. Highly recommended.

_____. "Story Tellers and Character: Point of View in Machado de Assis' Last Five Novels." *Latin American Literary Review* 7, no. 13 (Fall–Winter 1978):52–63. Shows that while Machado "allows the reader access to the implied author's processes of telling the story" (61), he also stresses the importance of the reader's active involvement in the story's interpretation. Argues that Machado makes the reader complete his novels in the ways indicated "by his subtle and withdrawn perspective on the subjects" (61). Calls Machado's five later novels exercises in "metaliterature" in which existence is characterized by irony, ambiguity, and self-love. Highly recommended.

Param, Charles. "Politics in the Novels of Machado de Assis." *Hispania* 56 (1973): 557–68. A sociopolitical and historical approach to Machado's novels; argues that Machado eschewed politics and that he "avoided controversy" of a political nature.

_____. "The Case for *Quincas Borba* as Confession." *Hispania* 50, no. 3 (September 1967):430–41. Param approaches this work from a generic perspective, that of the confession, and shows how this could alter our opinion of it; sees *Quincas Borba* as a "cathartic" novel, with Rubião a reflection of Machado himself.

_____. "Jealousy in the Novels of Machado de Assis." *Hispania* 53, no. 2 (May 1970):198–206. Focusing on one of Machado's major themes, or subthemes, Param shows how endemic this subject is to Machado's work in the novel form.

_____. "Machado de Assis and Dostoyevsky." *Hispania* 49, no. 1 (March 1966): 81–87. An interesting comparative study that, by focusing on certain themes and characters, shows how much Machado and Dostoyevski have in common.

Peixoto, Marta. "Aires as Narrator and Aires as Character in *Esaú e Jacó*." *Luso-Brazilian Review* 17, no. 1 (Summer 1980):79–92. A fine study of two crucial aspects of one of Machado's most overlooked masterpieces; highly recommended.

Pritchett, V. S. "Machado de Assis." *New Statesman,* 25 February 1966, 261–62. Contrasts the techniques of Machado's novels with those of his stories; also discusses Machado's approach to characterization and his essential modernity; says he has much in common with Pirandello.

Rabassa, Gregory. "A Minor Novel by a Major Writer." *New York Times Book Review,*

22 November 1970, 4. Notes the importance of a writer's "lesser novels" in terms of a great writer's development; discusses how *The Hand and the Glove,* Machado's second novel, anticipates the technical, thematic, and characterizational complexities of the later works.

Renshaw, Parke. "O humor em *Iaiá Garcia* e Brás Cubas." *Luso-Brazilian Review* 9, no. 1 (June 1972):13–20. The author compares and contrasts the nature and function of humor in these two works; calls *Iaiá Garcia* a romantic novel and the other a satire; believes that while there is little or no sarcasm in *Iaiá Garcia,* Brás Cubas is its living, breathing embodiment.

Sá Rego, Enylton de. "The Epic, the Comic and the Tragic: Tradition and Innovation in Three Late Novels of Machado de Assis." *Latin American Literary Review* 14, no. 27 (January–June 1986):19–34. Considers *Epitaph of a Small Winner* as a comic rewriting of the epic, *Philosopher or Dog?* as a tragic rewriting of the comic, and *Dom Casmurro* as a rewriting of tragedy.

Sena, Jorge de. "Machado de Assis and His Carioca Quintet." *Latin American Literary Review* 14, no. 27 (January–June 1986):9–18. Presents Machado's last five novels as an aesthetic whole in terms of the modern techniques of novelistic fiction; refers to *Dom Casmurro* as one of the masterpieces of the novel form.

Teixeira, Maria de Lourdes. "As mulheres machadianas." *Revista brasiliense* (São Paulo), no. 4 (March–April 1956):65–75. Compares Machado's most notable female characters; focuses especially on Capitú (*Dom Casmurro*), Sofia (*Quincas Borba*), and Carolina (Carmo, of *Counselor Ayres' Memorial*).

Turner, Doris M. "A Clarification of Some 'Strange' Chapters in Machado's *Dom Casmurro.*" *Luso-Brazilian Review* 13 (1976):55–66. The author, in quest of the novel's true "meaning," examines the following chapters, "The Worms," "The Opera," "A Sonnet," "A Dramatic Reform," "The Manduca Episode," and "O Barbeiro," and finds a thematic unity within them; they reflect and repeat each other.

Virgílio, Carmelo. "Love and the 'Causa Secreta' in the Tales of Machado de Assis." *Hispania* 49 (December 1966):778–86. Focuses on Machado's stories and discusses them primarily in terms of theme and characterization, the latter developed through comments on Machado's theory of literary characterization and his "pessimistic" worldview.

Weisberg, Richard. "Law in and as Literature: Self-Generated Meaning in the 'Procedural Novel.'" In *The Comparative Perspective in Literature,* edited by Clayton Koelb and Susan Noakes, pp. 224–32. Ithaca, N.Y.: Cornell University Press, 1988. The author, in attempting to deliniate the nature of this subgenre, discusses the crucial issues of narratorial reliability, the adversarial role of the narrator-as-protagonist-as-lawyer, and the role of the reader (as jury) in the establishing of meaning and textual veracity. Although he does not discuss any works by Machado de Assis, his commentaries of this kind of novel are very interesting in terms of what happens in *Dom Casmurro.*

Wilson, Clotilde. "Machado de Assis, Encomiast of Lunacy." *Hispania* 32 (May 1949):198–201. Focusing primarily on *Epitaph of a Small Winner* and *Philosopher or Dog?*, the author demonstrates Machado's preoccupation with insanity (especially megalomania) and shows how characters and themes in these two novels parallel the philosophy of Erasmus and the concerns of modern psychologists.

Ziomek, Henryk. "Parallel Ingredients in *Don Quixote* and *Dom Casmurro.*" *Revista de estudios hispánicos* 2 (1968):229–40. A good comparative study of these two works; focuses on a similar use of the "free indirect style," of ambiguous descriptions, of ironic names and titles, and of ironic, self-conscious narrators.

Index